IMPACT
CALIFORNIA SOCIAL STUDIES

Learning and Working
Now and Long Ago

RESEARCH COMPANION

Program Authors

James Banks, Ph.D.
Kerry and Linda Killinger Endowed Chair
in Diversity Studies
Director, Center for Multicultural Education
University of Washington
Seattle, Washington

Kevin P. Colleary, Ed.D.
Curriculum and Teaching Department
Graduate School of Education
Fordham University
New York, New York

William Deverell, Ph.D.
Director of the Huntington-USC Institute
on California and the West
Professor of History, University
of Southern California
Los Angeles, California

Daniel Lewis, Ph.D.
Dibner Senior Curator
The Huntington Library
Los Angeles, California

Elizabeth Logan, Ph.D., J.D.
Associate Director of the Huntington-
USC Institute on California and the West
Los Angeles, California

Walter C. Parker, Ph.D.
Professor of Social Studies Education
Adjunct Professor of Political Science
University of Washington
Seattle, Washington

Emily M. Schell, Ed.D.
Professor, Teacher Education
San Diego State University
San Diego, California

mheducation.com/prek-12

Send all inquiries to:
McGraw-Hill Education
303 E. Wacker Dr. Suite 2000
Chicago, IL 60601

ISBN: 978-0-07-899407-4
MHID: 0-07-899407-1

Printed in the United States of America.

2 3 4 5 6 QVS 21 20 19 18 17

Letter from the Authors

Dear Social Studies Detective,

How can we learn and work together? We learn at school. We work with people in our neighborhoods. How did people learn and work together long ago? In this book, you will read about learning and working today and long ago. You will also learn about being a great citizen!

As you read, be a detective. What do you wonder about? Write questions. Look for the answers! What are you interested in? Take notes about it. Do a project to share what you've learned. Take a closer look at photos of real people and places. Use maps to find your way!

Have fun while you investigate social studies and learn more about working and playing and learning together!

Sincerely,

The IMPACT Social Studies Author Team

WESTMINSTER RURAL POSTAL WAGON ROUTE—DELIVERING MAIL.

In the nineteenth century, mail was delivered using a horse and wagon.

Contents

Reference Sources

Good Citizens

How Do People Learn and Work Together

Our World

 Where Do We Live?

Our Country

What Does It Mean to Be an American?

Life Long Ago and Today

 How Has Our World Changed?

All About Work

 Why Do People Work?

Skills and Features

Maps

Primary Source Quotes

Getting Started

You have two social studies books.

The Inquiry Journal

This is your Inquiry Journal. It is where you ask questions and write answers.

The Research Companion

This is the Research Companion. It is where you look for clues and find answers.

Every Chapter

The chapter opener pages ask the **EQ,** an **essential question.** They also list the topics that you will learn about.

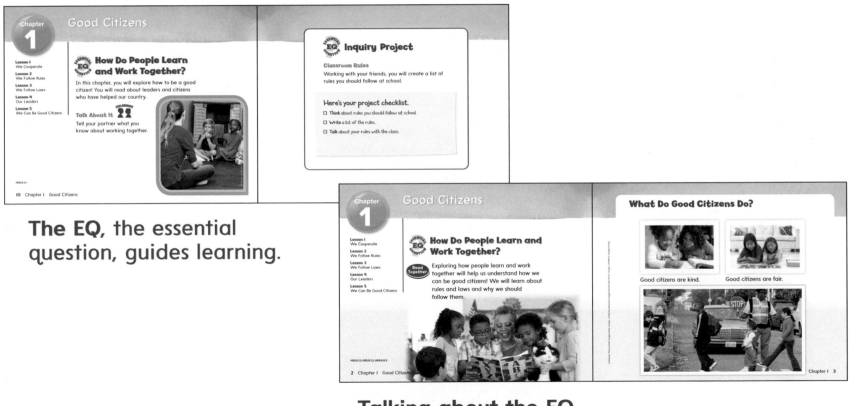

The EQ, the essential question, guides learning.

Talking about the EQ is a time to ask questions and share ideas.

Connect Through Literature

invites you to explore stories, poems, and other selections about people, places, and events in American history.

People You Should Know

helps you learn about the lives of people who have made a difference.

Every Lesson

Lessons start with a question. There is a picture for you to explore.

Learning **Outcomes** tell what you will learn and do in the lesson.

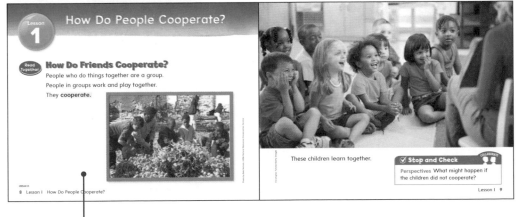

Lesson selections help you learn about the lesson topic and the EQ.

Analyze and Inquire

Investigate the essential question. Use your inquiry tools to look for answers.

Inquiry tools help you explore and organize new information.

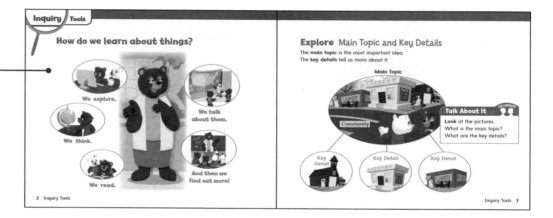

Primary Sources share the words and pictures of people from the past.

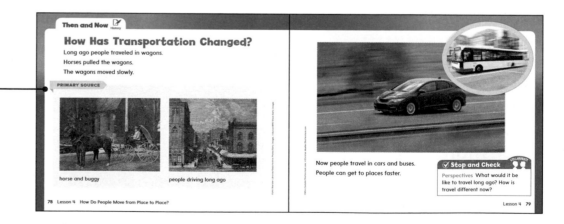

Report and Take Action

At the end of each lesson you can share your ideas about the EQ. Then you can choose an activity to show what you know.

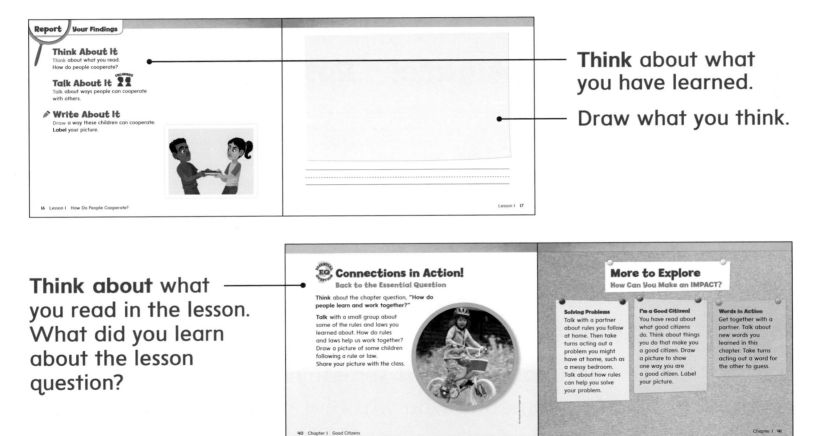

Think about what you have learned.

Draw what you think.

Think about what you read in the lesson. What did you learn about the lesson question?

Be a Social Studies Detective

How do you learn about people, places, and events? Become a Social Studies Detective!

Explore!   Investigate!   Report!

Look at Primary Sources

How do you learn about your world? You look for clues around you. Detectives explore and investigate too, just like you. One way that we can explore our world is by using primary sources.

What Is a Primary Source?

A primary source tells about or shows something that happened. It is told by someone who was there. Photographs and letters are primary sources. Diaries are primary sources too.

StasKhom/iStock/Getty Images

Look at the pictures. Ask questions.

Is it real?

Or is it make believe?

Is it a drawing?

Or is it a photo?

Talk About It

COLLABORATE

Look at the pictures. Which one is the real farmer? How do you know?

Look closely.

What do you see?

Talk About It

COLLABORATE

Who is in the picture? What are they doing? How do you know?

Look closely at the picture.

Is it a picture from now or long ago?

Find details that help you know.

Talk About It

COLLABORATE

What are the children in the picture doing? What detail in the picture is your clue?

Explore Geography

Geographers are detectives too.

They use maps and globes to find clues.

They ask questions about the world and where we live.

Using Maps

A map is a drawing of a place.

This is our country.

California is our state.

Talk About It

COLLABORATE

Look closely at the map.
Where is California?
What is near California?

The United States of America

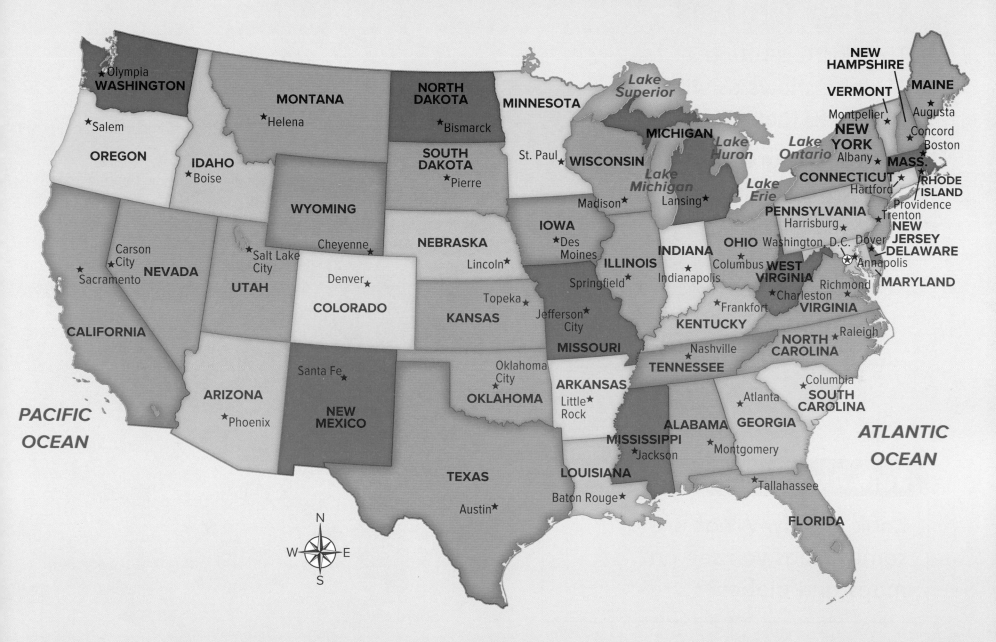

PACIFIC OCEAN

ATLANTIC OCEAN

WASHINGTON — ★Olympia, ★Salem

OREGON

IDAHO — ★Boise

MONTANA — ★Helena

NORTH DAKOTA — ★Bismarck

SOUTH DAKOTA — ★Pierre

MINNESOTA — St. Paul★

WISCONSIN — Madison★

MICHIGAN — Lansing★

Lake Superior

Lake Huron

Lake Michigan

Lake Ontario

Lake Erie

NEW HAMPSHIRE

VERMONT — Montpelier★

MAINE — ★Augusta

NEW YORK — Albany★

Concord★
Boston★

MASS.

CONNECTICUT — Hartford★

RHODE ISLAND — Providence★

PENNSYLVANIA — Harrisburg★

Trenton★
NEW JERSEY

NEVADA — Carson City★, ★Sacramento

UTAH — ★Salt Lake City

WYOMING — Cheyenne★

NEBRASKA — Lincoln★

IOWA — ★Des Moines

ILLINOIS — Springfield★

INDIANA — Indianapolis★

OHIO — Columbus★

Washington, D.C.

Dover★
DELAWARE

Annapolis★
MARYLAND

CALIFORNIA

COLORADO — Denver★

KANSAS — Topeka★

MISSOURI — Jefferson City★

WEST VIRGINIA — Charleston★

Richmond★
VIRGINIA

KENTUCKY — Frankfort★

ARIZONA — ★Phoenix

NEW MEXICO — Santa Fe★

OKLAHOMA — Oklahoma City★

ARKANSAS — Little Rock★

TENNESSEE — Nashville★

NORTH CAROLINA — Raleigh★

SOUTH CAROLINA — Columbia★

GEORGIA — Atlanta★

ALABAMA — Montgomery★

MISSISSIPPI — Jackson★

TEXAS — Austin★

LOUISIANA — Baton Rouge★

FLORIDA — Tallahassee★

N W E S

13a

Using Globes

The earth is round.
A globe shows us what
the Earth looks like.

The land is green.
The water is blue.

This is a globe.

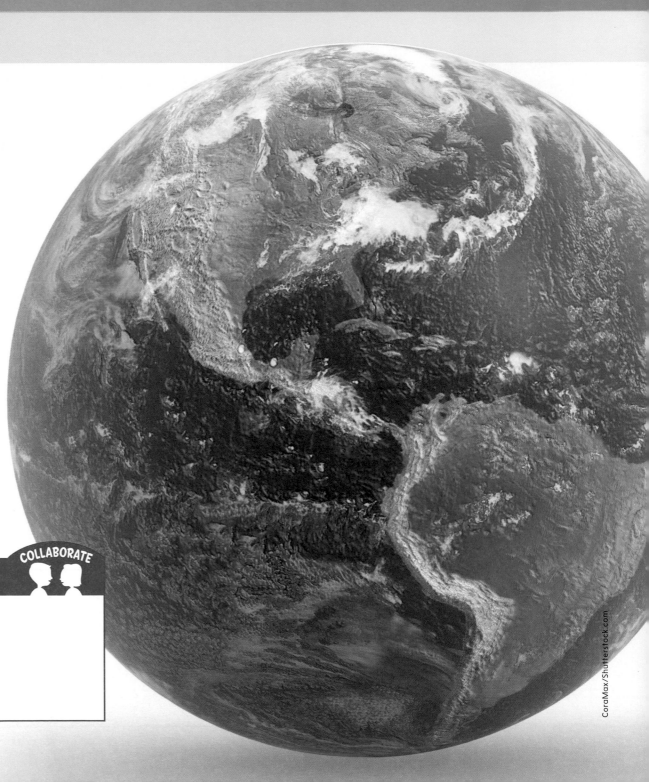

CoraMax/Shutterstock.com

Talk About It

COLLABORATE

Look closely. What are
some things you see on
maps and globes?

14a

North America

15a

Explore Economics

People have jobs. There are many different kinds of jobs. Jobs are important for communities.

Talk About It

COLLABORATE

What kinds of jobs are these people doing? What job do you want to have when you grow up?

People long ago had jobs too. Look closely.
What job are the people in this picture doing?

Explore Citizenship

Good citizens follow rules and help others. They make our world a better place.

The words on page 19a describe what it means to be a good citizen. We can be good citizens at home, at school, in our community, and in the world.

Take Action!

Social Studies Detectives ask questions. They look for clues. Clues help us learn about our world. We can all make an impact!

This firefighter works from up in the air to put out a fire.

Be a Good Citizen

COURAGE
Being brave

FREEDOM
Making our
own choices

HONESTY
Telling the truth

JUSTICE
Being fair
to everyone

LEADERSHIP
Showing good behavior
and being a good example

LOYALTY
Showing support for
people and one's country

RESPECT
Treating others as you
would like to be treated

RESPONSIBILITY
Being someone people can trust

Good Citizens

How Do People Learn and Work Together?

Exploring how people learn and work together will help us understand how we can be good citizens! We will learn about rules and laws and why we should follow them.

HSS.K.1.1, HSS.K.1.2, HSS.K.6.2

Getty Images/Blend Images

What Do Good Citizens Do?

Good citizens are kind.

Good citizens are fair.

Good citizens respect leaders and follow rules.

Connect Through Literature

Don't Throw It Away!

by Amy Tao, art by Sarah Beise

Paper, plastic, glass, and cans
Don't belong in the garbage can.

If you can't use them once again,
Toss 'em in the recycling bin.

Batteries, medicine, some cans that spray
Should not be just thrown away.

They're what's known as hazardous waste
And must be dumped in a special place.

Pile leaves and grass and vegetable scraps.
Abracadabra, zoom, and zap!

That compost heap will soon become
Plant food for your garden. Yum!

Toys and tools and clothes that are old
Can be given away or sold.

Reduce, recycle, and reuse.
We can all help Earth, if we choose.

Think About It

1. What are some things that we can recycle? What can we reuse?

2. Why is it important to recycle, reduce, and reuse?

People You Should Know

George Washington

George Washington was the first president of the United States. He did not want to be president, but our country needed a good leader. People thought George Washington would do a good job. He became the leader our country needed.

Iqbal Masih

Iqbal Masih was from Pakistan. He talked to people all over the world about children who needed our help. Iqbal made life better for many children.

Where in the World?

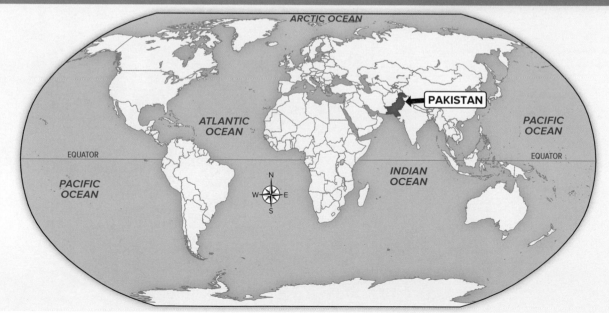

Lesson 1

How Do Friends Cooperate?

People who do things together are a group.

People in groups work and play together.

They **cooperate**.

Photo by Bob Nichols, USDA Natural Resources Conservation Service

HSS.K.1.1

These children learn together.

✓ **Stop and Check**

COLLABORATE

Perspectives What might happen if the children did not cooperate?

How Do Families Cooperate?

Families are a group too. They work together.

Jake lives with Dad and Aunt Sue.

They have work to do.

Jake and Aunt Sue rake the leaves.

Dad mows the lawn.

Jake, Dad, and Aunt Sue have fun too!

✓ **Stop and Check**   COLLABORATE

Talk What do Jake, Dad, and Aunt Sue do?
How do they help each other?

How Can We Show Respect?

Neighbors cooperate when they work together.

The neighborhood park is a mess!

The group has a job to do!

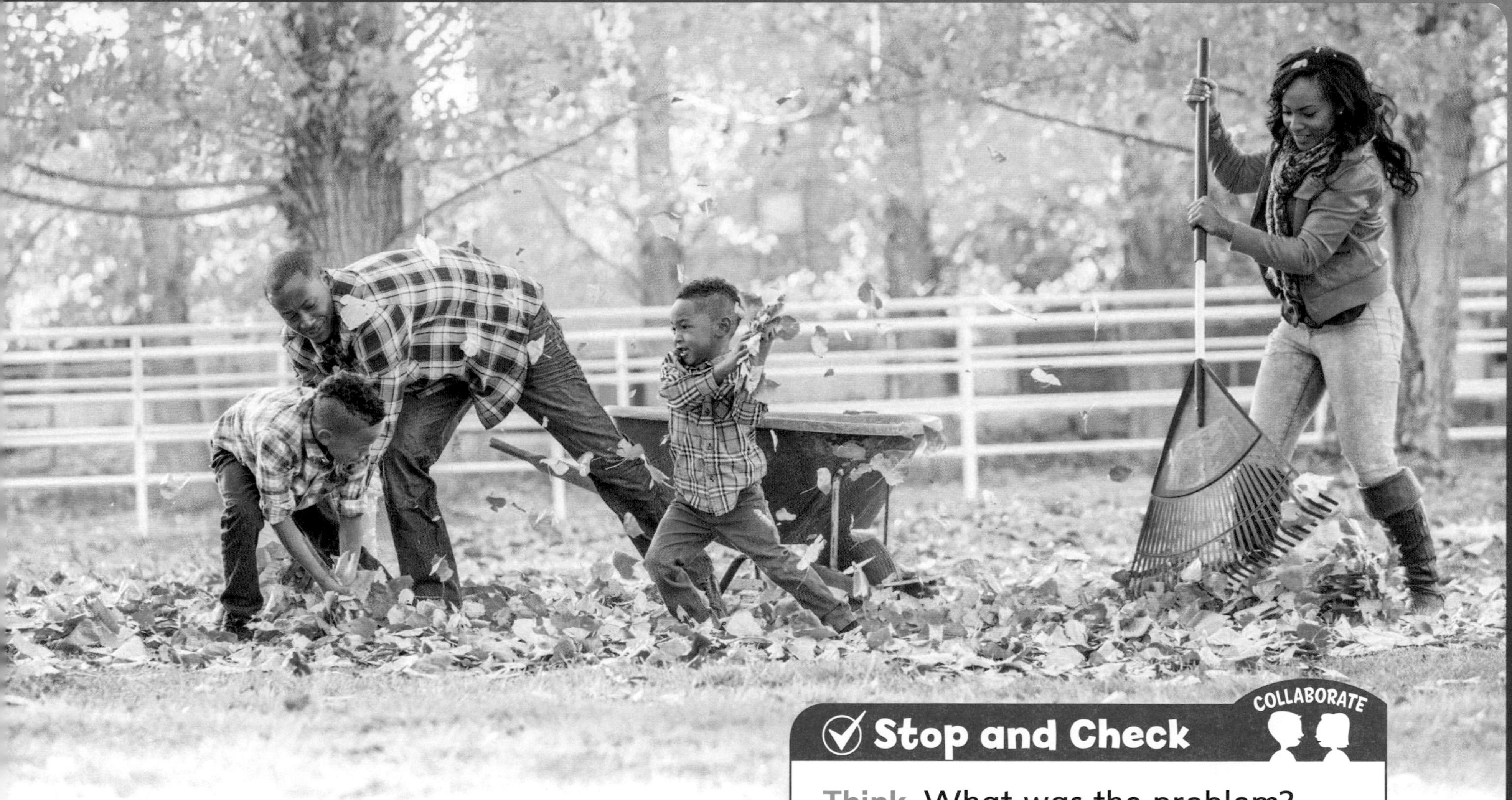

When we work together, there's so much we can do!

✔ **Stop and Check**

COLLABORATE

Think What was the problem? What did the people do? How did they work together?

What Do You Think?

How do people cooperate?

Lesson 2

Why Do We Have Rules?

Rules help people get along.

Rules tell us what we should do.

Rules help to keep people safe.

Rules are everywhere!

©Christopher Futcher/Getty Images

✓ Stop and Check

COLLABORATE

Talk What rules are the children following?

Perspectives Why are rules important?

What Happens When We Break Rules?

Rules also tell us what not to do.

✓ Stop and Check

Talk What does Goldilocks do?
What might happen to her after she breaks the rules?

Perspectives Why should we follow rules?

How Can We Solve Problems?

A problem is something you need to figure out.

To solve a problem means you find an answer.

There are three steps to solving a problem.

1. Name the problem.

2. List different choices.

3. Think and solve the problem.

Talk About It

COLLABORATE

Look at the picture.

How were they good problem solvers?

✓ Stop and Check

COLLABORATE

Perspectives How do you solve problems?

What Do You Think?

What are rules?

Why are they important?

Why Do People Have Laws?

What Are Laws?

A community makes **rules**.

These rules are called **laws**.

Laws help keep people safe.

A law may tell drivers to stop when people cross the street.

©Blend Images/Alamy

HSS.K.1.1, HSS.K.1.2, HSS.K.3, HSS.K.6.3, HAS.CS.3, HAS.HR.1

Laws tell you

- what you must do.
- what you cannot do.

A law may tell people to wear seat belts.

A law may tell people to wear bike helmets.

✓ Stop and Check

COLLABORATE

Talk How do these laws keep people safe?

Perspectives What might happen if people did not follow these laws?

What is Our Constitution?

The United States Constitution was written in 1787.

It has the most important laws for our country.

We follow these laws today.

How Have Laws Changed?

As times change, laws may need to change too.

Driving laws are different today than they were long ago.

People drove horses and buggies long ago.

Now people drive cars.

COLLABORATE

✓ Stop and Check

Talk Why did driving laws need to change?

How Do Community Workers Help Us?

Police officers direct traffic.

Crossing guards stop traffic at crosswalks.

(l)©McGraw-Hill Education/Christopher Kerrigan; (r)Steve Mason/Photodisc/Getty Images

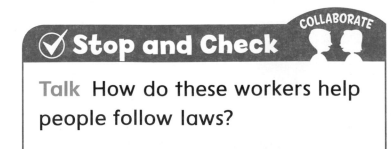

✓ Stop and Check

COLLABORATE

Talk How do these workers help people follow laws?

Who Is Malala Yousafzai?

epa european pressphoto agency b.v./Alamy

Many children in Pakistan were not allowed to go to school.

Malala knew that was not fair.

She worked to change the laws.

✓ Stop and Check   COLLABORATE

Talk What did Malala do? Why did she do it?

What Do You Think?

Why do people have laws?

Who Are Our Leaders?

Who Is the Leader of Our State?

The governor is the leader of California, our state.

The governor makes sure state **laws** are followed.

Jerry Brown

HSS.K.1.2, HSS.K.3, HSS.K.6.2

Who Is the Leader of Our Country?

The president is the leader of the United States.

The president works with other leaders to keep our country safe.

Donald Trump
45th U.S. President

Barack Obama
44th U.S. President

☑ Stop and Check COLLABORATE

Talk How are the governor and the president alike?
How are they different?

(t)Xirhua/Alamy Stock Photo; (b)Aarton Roeth Photography

The First President

George Washington was born long ago on a farm in Virginia.

At that time a country called England ruled America.

America had to follow England's laws.

The American people did not like this.

They went to war with England.

George Washington helped Americans win the war.

He was a hero.

The people of America made George our first president.

He is called the "Father of Our Country."

Yale University Art Gallery

George Washington riding a horse

Did You Know?

This is the Washington Monument.

The Washington Monument helps us remember our first president.

COLLABORATE

Stop and Check

Perspectives Do you think George Washington was a good leader? Why?

How Do Leaders Make Laws?

Some leaders think about the laws we need.

They work together to make these laws.

These leaders help make laws.

epa european pressphoto agency b.v./Alamy

Bettmann/Getty Images

Some leaders help us understand what laws mean.
They decide whether the laws are fair.
These leaders are called judges.

✓ Stop and Check

Talk How do some leaders help make laws?

What Do You Think?

Why are leaders important?

What Does It Mean to Be a Good Citizen?

What Is a Citizen?

A **citizen** is a member of a community.

You are a citizen at school.

You are a citizen of your town or city.

Disaster Relief

HSS.K.1.1

You are a citizen of your state.

You are a citizen of your country.

✓ Stop and Check

COLLABORATE

Talk What does it mean to be a citizen?

Make Connections How can you be a good citizen at school?

What Are Our Rights and Responsibilities?

Rights are things we all have.

Going to school is a right.

You have a right to be safe.

A **responsibility** is something a citizen should do.

You should do some community activities.

You should keep your community clean.

✓ Stop and Check

Make Connections What rights do you have? What responsibilities do you have?

How Can We Follow Rules?

We can follow **rules** at home.

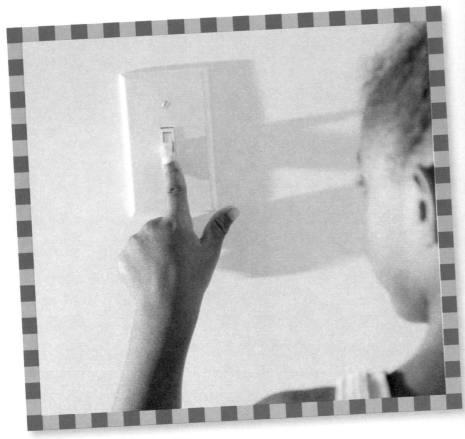

Turn off the lights when you leave the room.

Put your toys away.

We can follow rules at school.

We wait in line.

We listen.

✓ Stop and Check

COLLABORATE

Perspectives Why are rules important? What happens when people do not follow rules at home or at school?

How Can We Help?

We can help at school.

We can help at home.

FrareDavis Photography/Digital Vision/Getty Images

We can help in our community.

✓ **Stop and Check**

COLLABORATE

Perspectives Why is it important to help others?

What Do You Think?

What can you do to be a good citizen?

Connections in Action!
Back to the Essential Question

Think about the chapter question, **"How do people learn and work together?"**

Talk with a small group about some of the rules and laws you learned about. How do rules and laws help us work together? Draw a picture of some children following a rule or law.
Share your picture with the class.

Don Mason/Blend Images LLC

More to Explore

How Can You Make an IMPACT?

Solving Problems

Talk with a partner about rules you follow at home. Then take turns acting out a problem you might have at home, such as a messy bedroom. Talk about how rules can help you solve your problem.

I'm a Good Citizen!

You have read about what good citizens do. Think about things you do that make you a good citizen. Draw a picture to show one way you are a good citizen. Label your picture.

Words in Action

Get together with a partner. Talk about new words you learned in this chapter. Take turns acting out a word for the other to guess.

Chapter 2

Our World

ESSENTIAL **EQ** QUESTION

Where Do We Live?

Read Together

Exploring the world we live in will help us learn more about our neighborhood! We will learn about important places in our neighborhood. We will also learn about how we take care of our neighborhood.

HSS.K.1.2, HSS.K.3, HAS.HI.2

PhotoAlto/Alamy Stock Photo

Where in the World Do You Live?

There are many ways to name the places where you live.

Let's learn more about them! Your neighborhood is in your state. Your state is in a country. And your country is in the world!

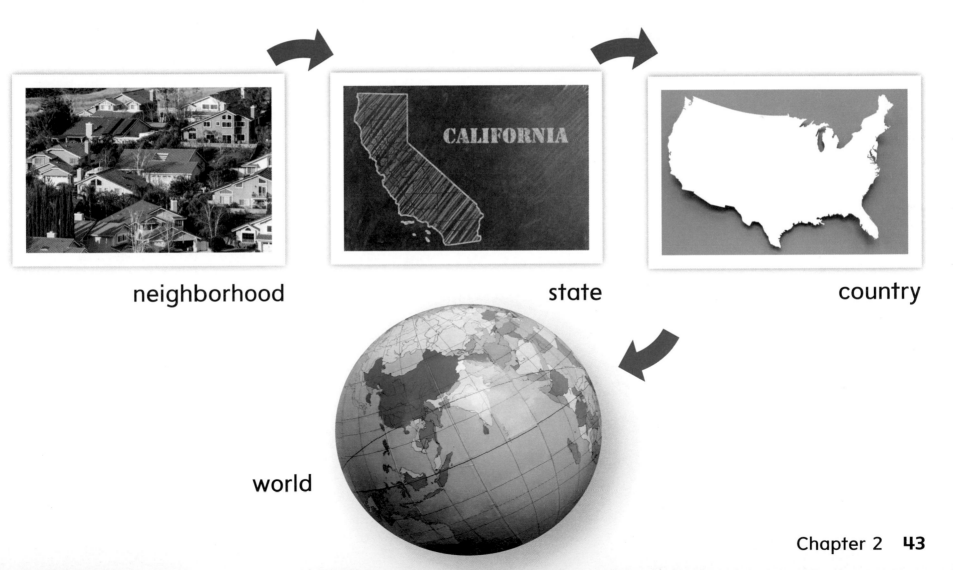

neighborhood

state

country

world

(tl)trekandshoot/iStock/Getty Images; (tc)Aaron Bastin/Alamy Stock Photo; (tr)Yuen Man Cheung/Alamy; (b)SukanPhoto/Shutterstock.com

Where My Aunt Rose Lives

by Eileen Spinelli,
art by Bonnie Gordon-Lucas

Where my Aunt Rose lives,
silver subways clatter past,
noisy factory whistles blast,
dented taxis travel fast,
where my Aunt Rose lives.

Where my Aunt Rose lives,
vendors sell hot dogs and hats,
firefighters rescue cats,
grandmas chat in laundromats,
where my Aunt Rose lives.

Where my Aunt Rose lives,
people soak up rooftop sun,
splash at hydrants just for fun,
order takeout by the ton,
where my Aunt Rose lives.

Where my Aunt Rose lives,
folks go dancing half the night,
parties everywhere in sight
in the twinkling city light,
where my Aunt Rose lives.

Where my Aunt Rose lives,

neighbors finally close their eyes,

first-floor baby wakes and cries,

distant trains hum lullabies,

where my Aunt Rose lives.

Think About It

1. Where does Aunt Rose live?

2. What can be seen where Aunt Rose lives? What can be heard there?

3. Would you like to live where Aunt Rose lives? Tell why or why not.

People You Should Know

Ellen Ochoa

Ellen Ochoa was the first Hispanic American woman to fly in a space shuttle. She is an astronaut. When she was traveling in space, she could see the whole world! She said, "I never got tired of watching the Earth . . . as we passed over it."

(t)NASA; (b)NASA/NOAA/GOES Project

Garbage Collectors

Garbage collectors are very important people! They pick up and remove garbage from our homes, schools, and parks. They help us take care of our world!

Go to School

Read Together

This is Sarah.

Sarah walks to school.
She lives near the school.

This is Juan.

They go to the same school.
Juan rides the bus to school.
He lives far away.

HSS.K.3, HSS.K.4.3, HSS.K.4.5, HAS.CS.4

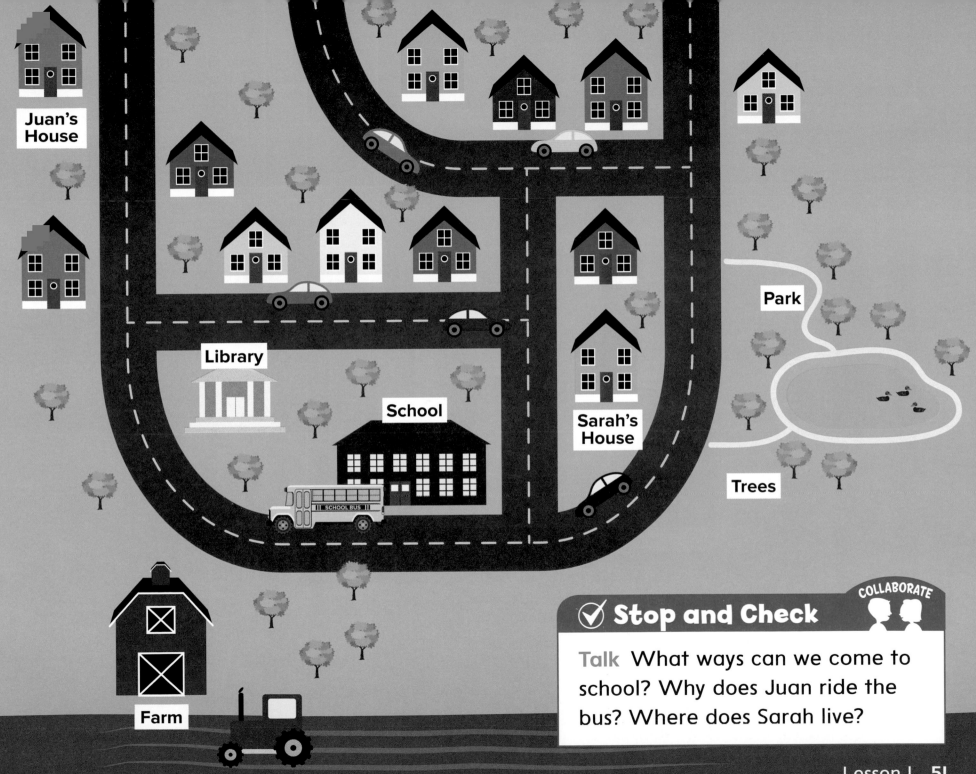

Juan's House

Library

School

SCHOOL BUS

Sarah's House

Park

Trees

Farm

✓ **Stop and Check**   COLLABORATE

Talk What ways can we come to school? Why does Juan ride the bus? Where does Sarah live?

Use the Map

Juan and Sarah use the **map**.

The map shows places in the school.

The map key tells them what the symbols mean.

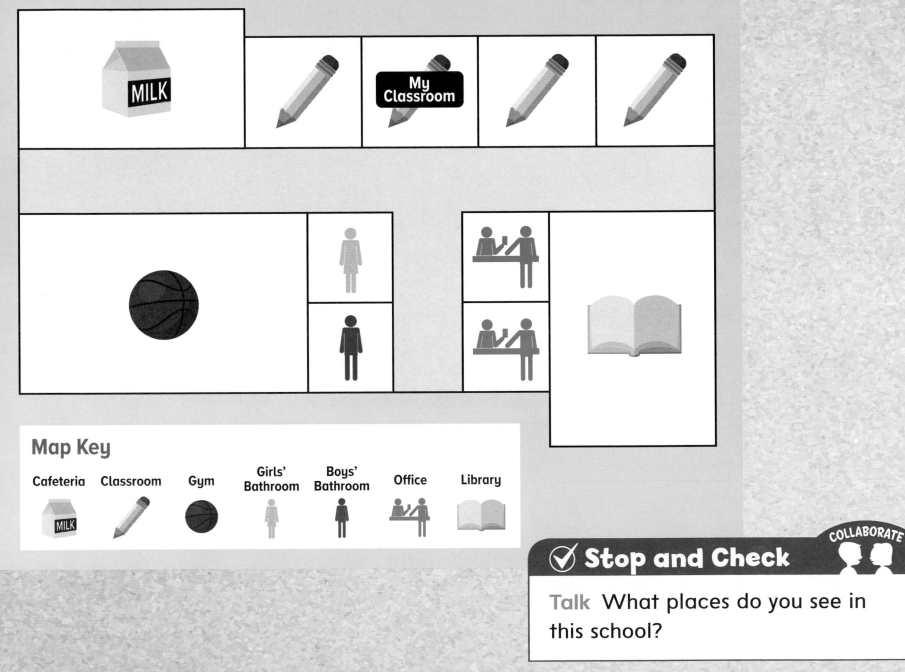

Map Key

| Cafeteria | Classroom | Gym | Girls' Bathroom | Boys' Bathroom | Office | Library |

✓ **Stop and Check** COLLABORATE

Talk What places do you see in this school?

School Workers

Many people work in the school.

They are called school workers.

They help all of the children learn.

Principal
The principal is the school leader.

Librarian
The librarian helps us find information.

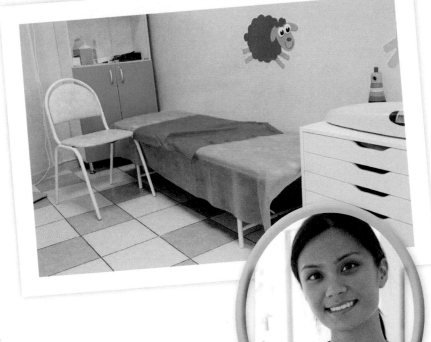

Teacher

Teachers make school fun and help students learn.

Nurse

The nurse helps students when they are sick.

✓ Stop and Check

COLLABORATE

Talk Who helps us at school?

How Do Children Get to School?

Peru

Peru

Some children in Peru get to school by boat.

China

China

Some children in China get to school by car.

(bkgd)Severe/Shutterstock.com; (l)FionaMark/iStock/Getty Images; (r)RonTech2000/iStock/Getty Images

Some children in the United States get to school by bus.

Some children in France skate to school.

✓ Stop and Check

COLLABORATE

Talk How do children around the world get to school?

What Do You Think?

What can we find at our school?

What Is a Neighborhood?

Read Together

What Do Maps and Globes Show?

A **globe** is a model of the Earth.

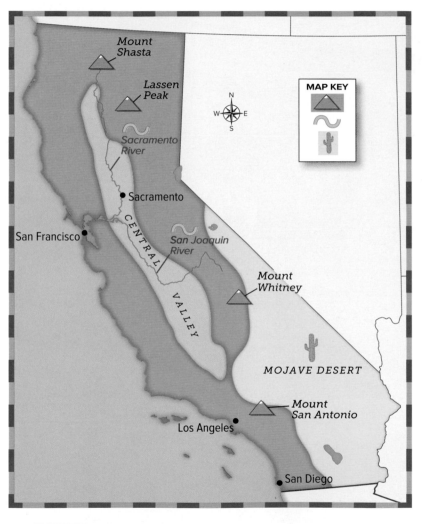

MAP KEY

Mount Shasta
Lassen Peak
Sacramento River
Sacramento
San Francisco
CENTRAL VALLEY
San Joaquin River
Mount Whitney
MOJAVE DESERT
Mount San Antonio
Los Angeles
San Diego

©McGraw-Hill Education/Janette Beckman

A **map** is a drawing of a place. This is a map of California.

HSS.K.4.2, HSS.K.4.3, HSS.K.4.4, HAS.CS.4, HAS.HI.2

Map and Globe Skills

Maps use symbols to show landforms.

A river has this symbol.

A desert has this symbol.

A mountain has this symbol.

(bkgd)McGraw-Hill Education; (l)John Alves/Getty Images; (c)Pamela Long/Moment/Getty Images; (r)Christopher Boswell/Shutterstock.com

✓ Stop and Check

COLLABORATE

Talk Where are the landforms on the map? What color is the water on the globe? What color is the land?

What Are Neighborhoods Like?

A **neighborhood** is a place where people live and work.

People live here.

People work here.

There are many kinds of neighborhoods.

This is a farm.

This is a city.

✓ **Stop and Check**

Make Connections What kind of neighborhood do you live in?

(inset)Marco Colorizio/Digital Vision/Getty Images; (bkgd Disorderly/iStock/Getty Images

What Is in a Neighborhood?

A neighborhood has many important places.

fire station

police station

post office

grocery
store

library

hospital

✓ Stop and Check   COLLABORATE

Talk What are important places
in a neighborhood?

How Do I Get Around My Neighborhood?

I walk and ride my bike.

I walk to school every day.

I ride my bike to the park.

(bkgd)McGraw-Hill Education; (inset)Jupiterimages/Stockbyte/Getty Images

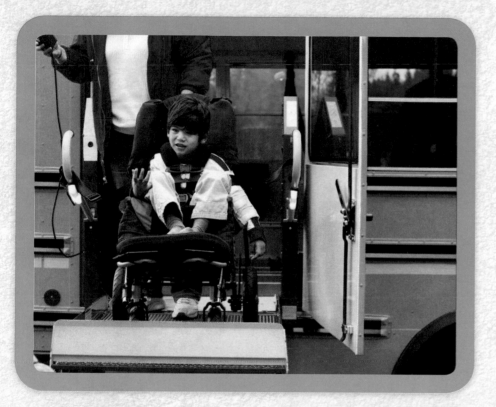

I use my wheelchair.

Curbs and steps can make it hard.

Ramps and other things help me.

This lift helps me.

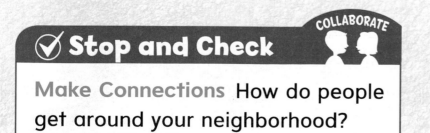

✓ Stop and Check

COLLABORATE

Make Connections How do people get around your neighborhood?

What Do You Think?

What is a neighborhood?

Read Together Where Is Our Neighborhood?

Our **neighborhood** is part of a **state**.

Hollywood, California

San Jose, California

Sausalito, California

HSS.K.4.1, HSS.K.4.2, HSS.K.4.3, HAS.CS.4

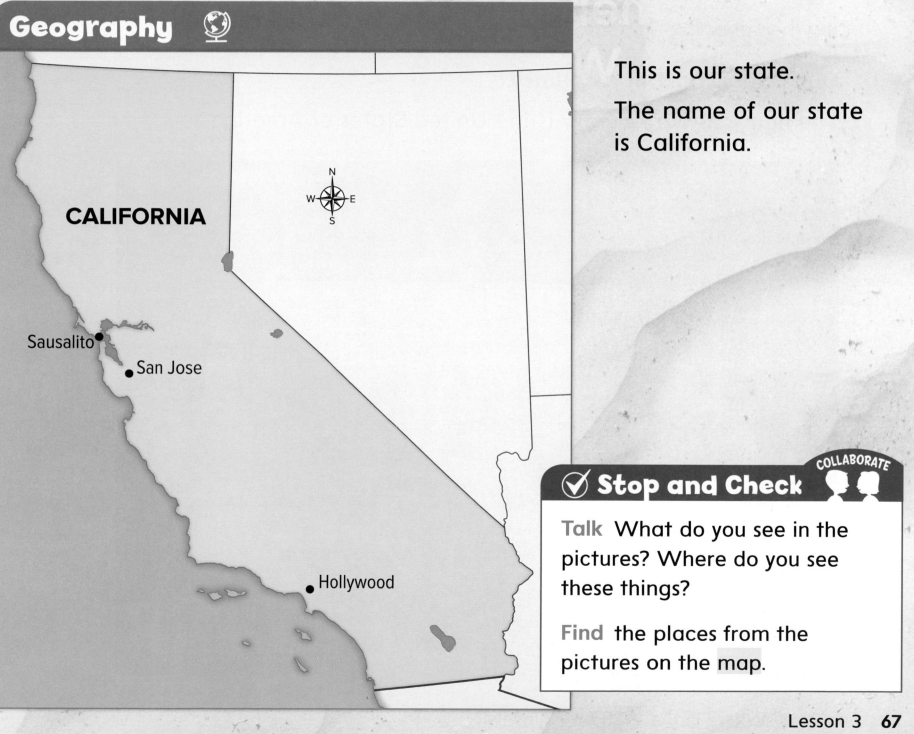
This is our state.

The name of our state is California.

CALIFORNIA

N
W
E
S

Sausalito

San Jose

Hollywood

✓ Stop and Check COLLABORATE

Talk What do you see in the pictures? Where do you see these things?

Find the places from the pictures on the map.

Where Is Our State?

Our state is part of a **country**.

The name of our country is the United States of America.

Adam Hester/Blend Images/Getty Images

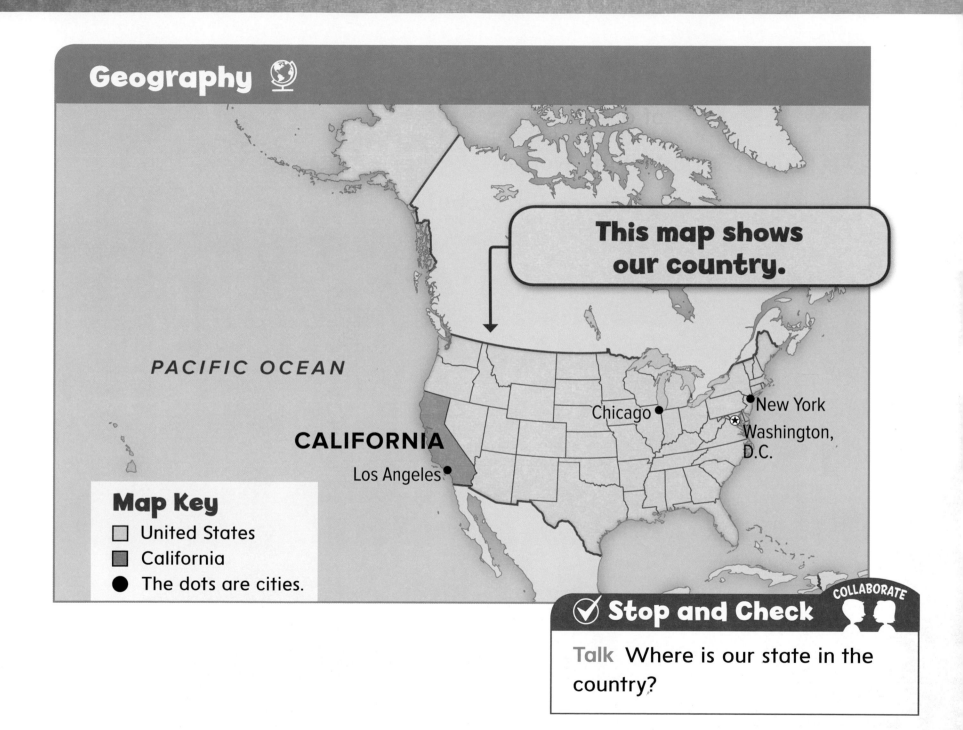

This map shows our country.

PACIFIC OCEAN

CALIFORNIA

Los Angeles •

Chicago •

• New York

⭐ Washington, D.C.

Map Key
☐ United States
▨ California
● The dots are cities.

✓ **Stop and Check** COLLABORATE

Talk Where is our state in the country?

Where Is Our Country?

Our country is part of the **world**.

Can you find our country on this globe?

D. Hurst/Alamy

This is our world.

There are countries all around the world.

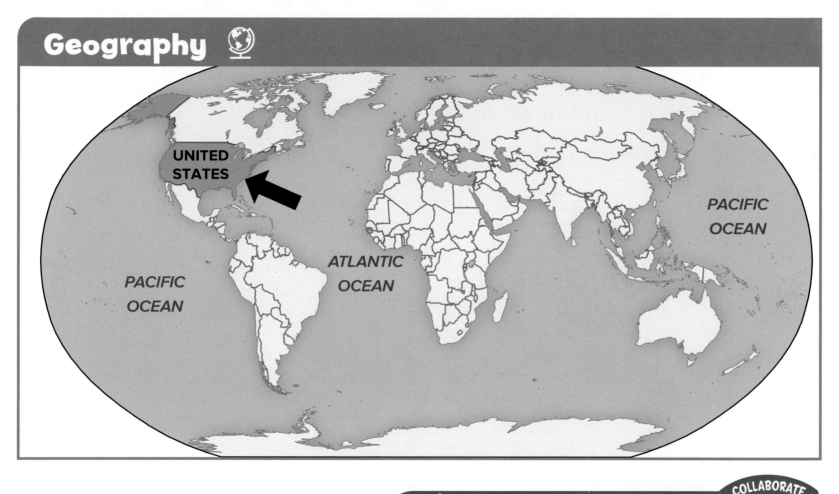

UNITED STATES

PACIFIC OCEAN

ATLANTIC OCEAN

PACIFIC OCEAN

✓ Stop and Check

Talk Where is our country in the world? What is around our country?

Where Do People Live?

There are many places in the world.

Some places have special homes.

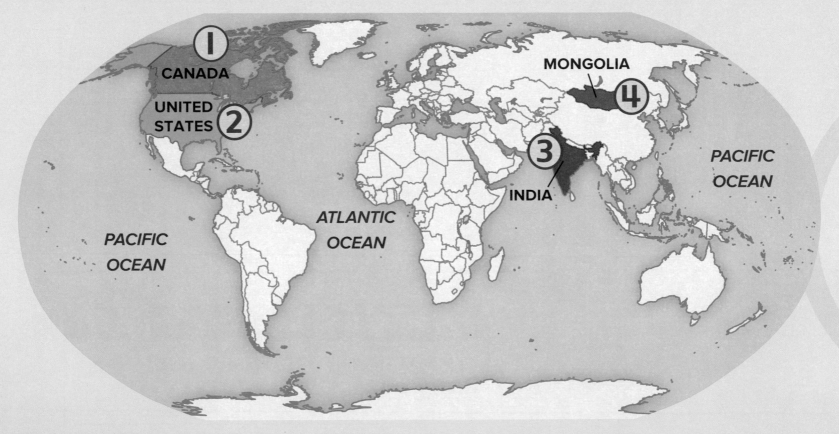

CANADA ①

UNITED STATES ②

MONGOLIA ④

③ INDIA

PACIFIC OCEAN

ATLANTIC OCEAN

PACIFIC OCEAN

①

Canada

②

United States

③

India

④

Mongolia

✓ Stop and Check

COLLABORATE

Perspectives What would it be like to live in these homes? What is your home like?

What Do You Think?

Where in the world do we live?

Read Together

How Can We Use Map Symbols?

Maps have symbols.

The symbols help us find things.

A map key tells what each symbol means.

Map Key

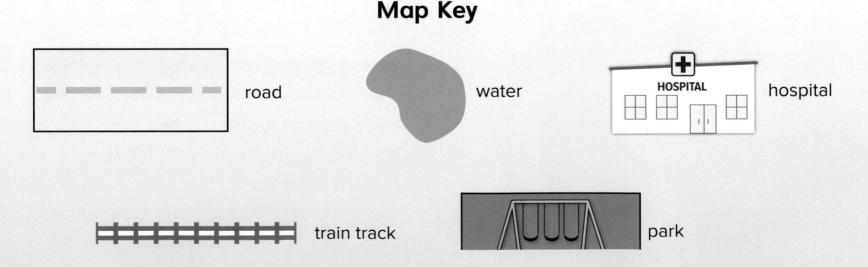

road

water

hospital

train track

park

HSS.K.1.2, HSS.K.4.1, HSS.K.4.2, HSS.K.4.3, HSS.K.6.2, HSS.K.6.3, HAS.CS.1, HAS.CS.3, HAS.CS.4, HAS.CS.5, HAS.HI.1

This is a map of a **neighborhood**.

What is in the neighborhood?

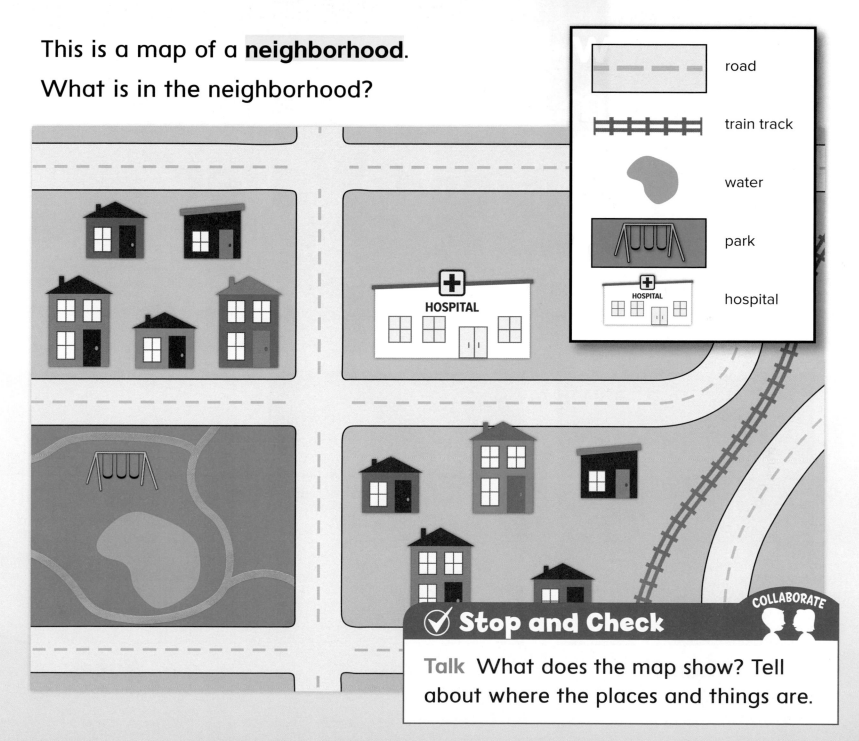

	road
	train track
	water
	park
	hospital

✓ Stop and Check COLLABORATE

Talk What does the map show? Tell about where the places and things are.

How Do People Move over Land, Air, and Water?

A chart shows information.

This chart shows different kinds
of transportation people can use.

Land   **Air**   **Water**

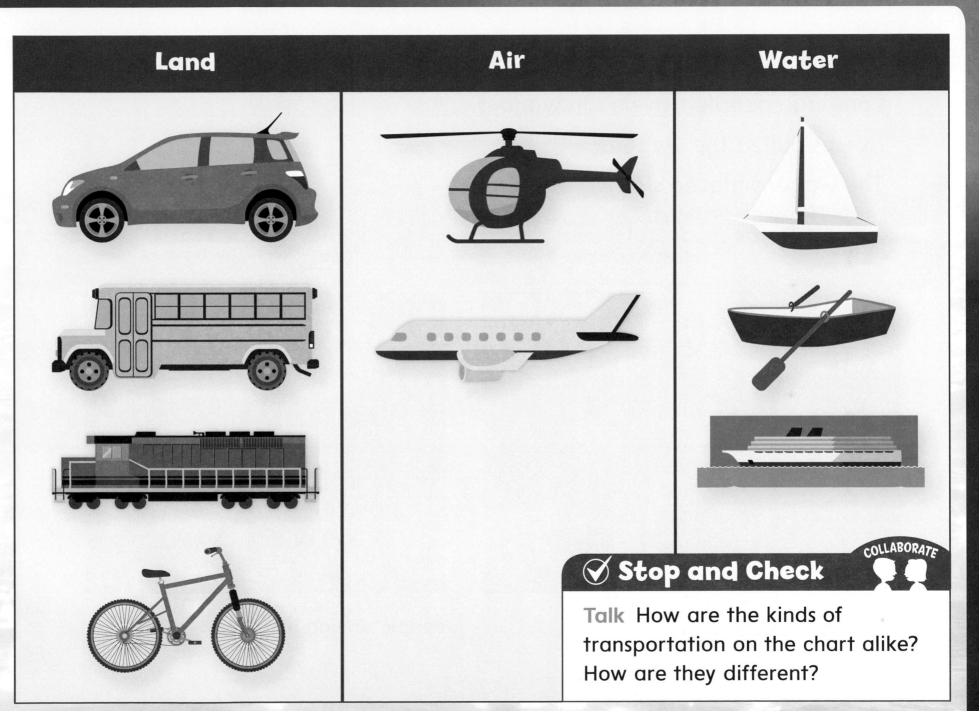

Land	Air	Water

Stop and Check COLLABORATE

Talk How are the kinds of transportation on the chart alike? How are they different?

How Has Transportation Changed?

Long ago people traveled in wagons.

Horses pulled the wagons.

The wagons moved slowly.

PRIMARY SOURCE

horse and buggy

people driving long ago

Now people travel in cars and buses.

People can get to places faster.

✅ **Stop and Check**

COLLABORATE

Perspectives What would it be like to travel long ago? How is travel different now?

Who Was Daniel Boone?

Daniel Boone lived a long time ago.

He liked to travel and explore.

But it was hard to travel to some places.

Daniel Boone helped people travel.

(bkgd)Pat & Chuck Blackley/Alamy

Daniel Boone helped make a new path.

The path was called Wilderness Road.

The path made travel easier.

Did You Know?

You can still walk on Wilderness Road.

It is part of a park in Virginia.

✓ Stop and Check

COLLABORATE

Perspectives Why was it a good idea to make Wilderness Road?

What Do You Think?

How do people move from place to place?

Read Together

How Can We Reuse Materials?

We can reuse things.

We can take something old.

We can use it to make something new.

You can make a bird feeder!

HSS.K.1.2, HSS.K.1.3, HSS.K.4.2, HSS.K.6.2, HAS.CS.1, HAS.CS.4, HAS.HR.3

How to Mak a Bird Feed r

1. Cut a hole.

2. Add a stick.

3. Decorate.

4. Add string.

> ✓ **Stop and Check** COLLABORATE
>
> **Make Connections** How can you reuse things? Why is it important to reuse things?

What Is the Legend of Johnny Appleseed?

Johnny Appleseed lived a long time ago.

He wore a pot for a hat!

He had animal friends.

Johnny Appleseed walked across the **country**.

He planted seeds.

The seeds grew into apple trees!

Did You Know?

Trees are important to Earth.

They make the air clean!

✓ **Stop and Check** COLLABORATE

Talk How did Johnny Appleseed help take care of Earth?

Who was John Chapman?

John Chapman, also known as Johnny Appleseed, lived a long time ago.

He planted seeds in different places.

The seeds grew into apple trees.

John Chapman

Where Did John Chapman Go?

Look at the **map**.

Where did John Chapman plant apple seeds?

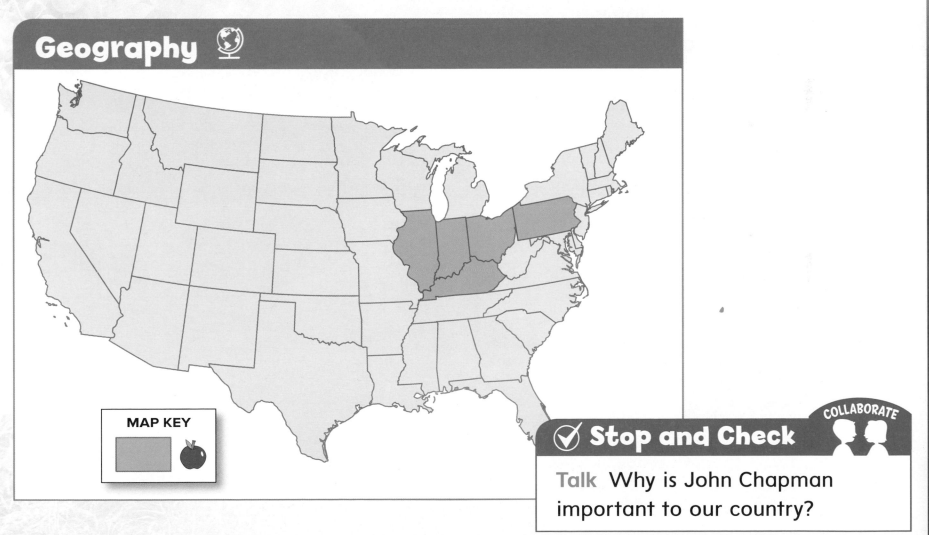

Geography 🌐

MAP KEY

✓ Stop and Check

Talk Why is John Chapman important to our country?

Why Should We Be Global Citizens?

We can take care of our **world**.

We do not waste.

We keep it clean.

(l)©Creatas/PunchStock, (r)thislife pictures/Alamy

We learn about other people.

We care for each other.

Together we can make the world
a better place!

✓ Stop and Check

Perspectives Why is it important
to care for our world?

What Do You Think?

How can you take care of your
neighborhood?

Connections in Action!

Back to the Essential Question

Think about the chapter question, **"Where do we live?"**

Talk with a partner about some of the places you learned about in this chapter. What do you know about where you live? Share your ideas with the class.

More to Explore
How Can You Make an IMPACT?

My Word Book

Think of three new words you learned in this chapter. Draw a picture that shows the meaning of each word. Copy the word to label your picture. Then put the pages together. Share your word book with the class!

Neighborhood Places

Build a model of your neighborhood. Include important places you have learned about. Use blocks, toys, and other objects in the classroom. Then share your model with the class. Talk about the important places.

Make a List

You've read about places in your neighborhood and around the world. Draw one place you read about. List two things you know about that place. Share your list with a partner. Talk about why the place is important.

Our Country

What Does It Mean to Be an American?

Exploring our country will help us learn what it means to be an American! We will learn about heroes from our country. We will learn about how we can be heroes too!

HSS.K.1.2, HSS.K.2, HSS.K.6.2,
HAS.CS.4

Adam Hester/Blend Images/Alamy

This Is Our Country

Our country is the United States of America. It has 50 states. Our state is California. California is on the left side of our country.

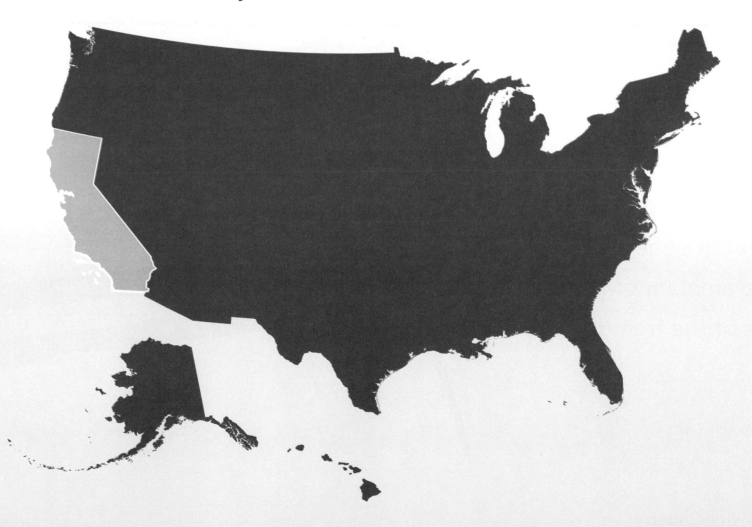

VectorShots/Shutterstock.com

You're a Grand Old Flag

by George M. Cohan

You're a grand old flag,

You're a high flying flag

And forever in peace may you wave.

You're the emblem of the land I love.

The home of the free and the brave.

Glow Images

Ev'ry heart beats true
'neath the Red, White,
and Blue,

Where there's
never a boast or brag.

Should auld acquaintance
be forgot,

Keep your eye
on the grand old flag.

TEXT: Cohan, George M. "You're a Grand Old Flag." New York: F. A. Mills, 1906. Library of Congress [M1508.GeorgeWashingtonJr].; PHOTO: Ariel Skelley/Blend Images/Getty Images

Think About It

1. What flag is this song about?
   How do you know?

2. How do you think the person who
   wrote this song feels about the flag?
   Tell why you think so.

People You Should Know

Booker T. Washington

Booker T. Washington was a teacher long ago. Many schools did not teach African Americans then. Washington knew that school was important. He helped start a school for African Americans.

Clara Barton

Long ago there was a war in our country. Clara Barton took care of people. She gave them food and clothing. After the war Clara wanted to keep helping people. She worked for the Red Cross. The Red Cross helps people all over the world.

(l)Ilene MacDonald/Alamy; (r)kittimages/iStockphoto/Getty Images; (inset)Library of Congress Prints and Photographs Division [LC-USZ62-19319]

Why Are National Symbols Important?

Read Together

What Is Our Country's Song?

Many people live in the United States.

Together we make one country.

We are proud of our country.

We are proud of our flag.

We have a song called
The Star Spangled Banner.

Joanne Stemberger/iStockphoto/Getty Images

✓ Stop and Check

Think What symbol is the song about?

Why Is the Bald Eagle Important?

The bald eagle is a symbol of our country.

It is big and strong. Our country is big and strong, too.

Gordon Pusnik/EyeEm/Getty Images

The bald eagle stands for freedom.

It also stands for strength.

It makes us feel proud
to be Americans.

Did You Know?

The bald eagle
is on mailboxes
and mail
trucks, too.

✓ Stop and Check

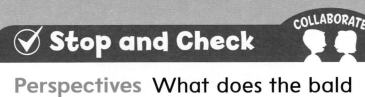

Perspectives What does the bald
eagle tell you about our country?

Where else do you see symbols?

Coins are round pieces of metal.

They are used as money.

In the United States, the coins have symbols of our country.

This is a quarter.

The name of our country.

George Washington

What symbols do you see?

✓ Stop and Check

COLLABORATE

Perspectives What do symbols tell you about our country?

Why Is the Statue of Liberty Important?

The Statue of Liberty was a gift to America.

It came from France.

It was so big, it had to be sent in hundreds of pieces!

PRIMARY SOURCE

The Statue of Liberty is a symbol of freedom.
It stands for hope.
It has welcomed people to our country
for a long time.
The statue is in New York Harbor.

✓ Stop and Check

COLLABORATE

Perspectives Why is the Statue of Liberty important to our country?

What Do You Think?

Why are symbols important to our country?

Read Together

What Is Labor Day?

A **holiday** is a special day.

Some holidays celebrate our **nation**.

This poster represents women who worked in America over 70 years ago.

National Archives and Records Administration (NWDNS-179-WP-1563)

SEPTEMBER

Sunday	Monday	Tuesday	Wednesday	Thursday	Friday	Saturday
	1	2	3	4	5	6
7	8	9	10	11	12	13
14	15	16	17	18	19	20
21	22	23	24	25	26	27
28	29	30				

Labor Day is a holiday in September.

Labor Day celebrates the great things workers do for our **country**.

COLLABORATE

✓ Stop and Check

Talk What are holidays? Why do we celebrate Labor Day?

Perspectives Why are workers important in our nation?

What Is Independence Day?

Independence Day is a holiday.

It celebrates the birth of the United States of America. It is also called the Fourth of July. We celebrate with parades and fireworks.

JULY						
Sunday	Monday	Tuesday	Wednesday	Thursday	Friday	Saturday
		1	2	3	4	5
6	7	8	9	10	11	12
13	14	15	16	17	18	19
20	21	22	23	24	25	26
27	28	29	30	31		

✓ Stop and Check COLLABORATE

Talk What is Independence Day? What do people do to celebrate?

Make Connections How does your community celebrate Independence Day?

Who Is Abraham Lincoln?

Abraham Lincoln was an important president.

Lincoln always tried to tell the truth.
People called him Honest Abe.

We celebrate his birthday February 12th.

Abraham Lincoln

Sunday	Monday	Tuesday	Wednesday	Thursday	Friday	Saturday
			1	2	3	4
5	6	7	8	9	10	11
12	13	14	15	16	17	18
19	20	21	22	23	24	25
26	27	28				

FEBRUARY

Who Is George Washington?

George Washington was our first president.

On February 22, we celebrate his birthday.

We remember what he did for our country.

(l)©Comstock Images/Alamy; (inset)Yale University Art Gallery

George Washington

✓ **Stop and Check**

COLLABORATE

Talk Whose birthday comes first? Why do we celebrate Washington's and Lincoln's birthdays?

How Do We Remember Our Heroes?

On Memorial Day, we honor soldiers who have fought and died for the United States.

It is celebrated on the last Monday of May.

Sunday	Monday	Tuesday	Wednesday	Thursday	Friday	Saturday
	1	2	3	4	5	6
7	8	9	10	11	12	13
14	15	16	17	18	19	20
21	22	23	24	25	26	27
28	29	30	31			

MAY

Memorial Day is in May.

On Veterans Day, we celebrate veterans.

A veteran is a person who has protected our country.

A veteran is a hero.

We celebrate Veterans Day on November 11th.

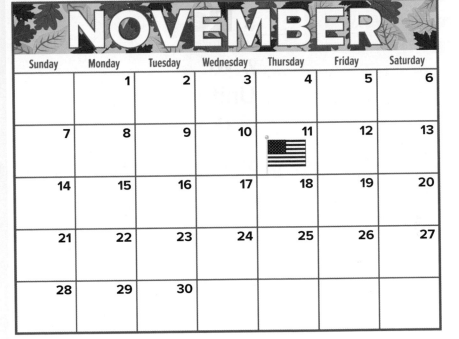

NOVEMBER						
Sunday	Monday	Tuesday	Wednesday	Thursday	Friday	Saturday
	1	2	3	4	5	6
7	8	9	10	11	12	13
14	15	16	17	18	19	20
21	22	23	24	25	26	27
28	29	30				

Veterans Day is in November.

✓ Stop and Check

COLLABORATE

Talk Why do we celebrate Memorial Day and Veterans Day?

What Do You Think?

How do people celebrate America?

Read Together

What Are Special Places in Our Country?

This is the White House.
It is located in Washington D.C.,
our country's capital.

HSS.K.1.2, HSS.K.2, HSS.K.6.2, HAS.HR.1, HAS.HR.2, HAS.HI.1, HAS.HI.2, HAS.HI.3

114   Lesson 3   How Do People and Places Help Us Learn About America?

Getty Images/iStockphoto

The president lives here.

The president works here too.

The president's office is shaped like an oval!

✓ **Stop and Check**

Talk What questions do you have about the White House? Why is the White House a special place?

Field Trip to Philadelphia

The Liberty Bell is another symbol.
It rang long ago when the United States became a country.
The Liberty Bell is famous for its big crack.
Many people visit it everyday.

Did You Know?

No one knows how the Liberty Bell had its first crack.

The Liberty Bell is in Philadelphia, Pennsylvania.

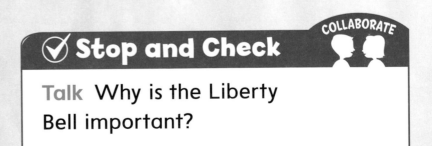

✓ **Stop and Check** COLLABORATE

Talk Why is the Liberty
Bell important?

A Great President

Abraham Lincoln was born in 1809.

He taught himself to read and write.

Abraham Lincoln was a President of the United States.

He was one of our greatest presidents. Lincoln helped keep our country together during the Civil War.

penny

(t bl)©McGraw-Hill Education/Ken Cavanagh; (bp)Library of Congress Prints and Photographs Division (LC-USZ62-7990)

Abraham
Lincoln

Lincoln Memorial

Did You Know?

Abraham Lincoln was the first
president to make Thanksgiving a
national holiday.

How Do Ben Franklin's Ideas Help Us?

People with great ideas help make our work and lives better.

Benjamin Franklin was a person with great ideas.

Ben Franklin was an inventor.

He made many helpful things.

He discovered helpful things too.

bifocals

electricity

(l)Ingram Publishing/SuperStock; (r)©Comstock Images/Alamy; (inset)Library of Congress Prints and Photographs Division (LC-USZ62-307501)

lightning rod

Franklin stove

☑ Stop and Check

COLLABORATE

Talk What did Ben Franklin make? What did he find out? How do his inventions help us?

What Do You Think?

How do we learn about our country?

How Do We Celebrate California?

What Symbols Represent Our State?

We are proud of our **state**!

We have special **symbols** to show we are proud.

California poppy

California quarter

California red-legged frog

California grizzly bear

California quail

Did You Know?

The California state colors are blue and gold.

✓ Stop and Check

COLLABORATE

Perspectives What do these symbols tell you about our state?

Tall, Tall Trees

Look outside. Do you see a tree?

It might be tall.

It is not as tall as a redwood called a giant sequoia!

These huge redwoods can be as tall as a 30-story building.

One tree can weigh as much as 100 elephants.

The trees live for a long time, too.

Some of them have been alive for more than 1,000 years.

These special trees grow only in California.

A giant sequoia
really is giant!

✓ **Stop and Check** COLLABORATE

Talk What makes these trees special?

Cesar Chavez

Cesar Chavez was born in 1927.

When Cesar was young, he and his family were farm workers.

They were not paid very much money.

MARCH						
Sunday	Monday	Tuesday	Wednesday	Thursday	Friday	Saturday
			1	2	3	4
5	6	7	8	9	10	11
12	13	14	15	16	17	18
19	20	21	22	23	24	25
26	27	28	29	30	31	

Anacleto Rapping/Los Angeles Times/Getty Images

People walk to remember Cesar Chavez.

People did not treat farm workers fairly.

Cesar Chavez worked for new laws.

The laws help keep farm workers safe.

✓ Stop and Check

COLLABORATE

Perspectives How do you think farm workers felt when Cesar Chavez helped them?

What Do You Think?

How do we celebrate California?

How Do We Show Pride in Our Nation?

What Is a Hero?

A **hero** is determined.

A hero is honest.

A hero is brave.

(tr)Ted Foxx/Alamy; (l)©Hero/age fotostock; (br)©Ariel Skelley/Blend Images LLC

A hero is respectful.

A hero is patriotic.

A hero is responsible.

✓ Stop and Check

Perspectives Why is it important to be a hero?

Make Connections How can you be a hero?

Respecting Our Nation

To respect means to treat as important.

We show respect for our nation
by keeping it clean.

How can we help?

We can help our community!

We can give food.

DONATIONS

We can plant trees.

We can take care of animals.

✓ Stop and Check

Make Connections How can you help your community?

How Can We Cooperate?

We can work together!

We can clean up together.

We can build together.

We can play together too!

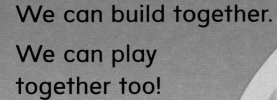

✓ Stop and Check

COLLABORATE

Perspectives How does working together show we are proud of our country?

How Can We Show Courage?

When you show **courage**, it means you are brave.

We can show courage every day.

We can try something new.

We can make new friends.

We can do the right thing.

✓ Stop and Check

COLLABORATE

Perspectives Why does doing these things show courage? What are some other ways we can show courage?

What Do You Think?

How do we show pride in our nation?

Connections in Action!
Back to the Essential Question

Think about the chapter question, **"What does it mean to be an American?"**

Talk with a partner about some of the people and places you learned about. How do they help you understand our country? Draw a picture that represents our country. Share your picture with the class.

Photo by John Crouch/Moment Select/Getty Images

More to Explore

How Can You Make an IMPACT?

Which Word?

Choose two new words you learned in this chapter. Draw a picture that shows the meaning of each word. Then trade pictures with a partner. Tell which words from the chapter your partner's pictures show. Label each picture with the word.

Our State

You've learned about our state in this chapter. What is the most interesting thing you learned? Draw a picture to show an interesting detail about our state. Share your picture with a partner. Tell why you picked this detail.

I Can Be a Hero!

You've learned about what heroes do. Get together with a partner. Role-play ways you can be a hero. Choose your favorite idea to share with your class.

Life Long Ago and Today

ESSENTIAL EQ QUESTION

How Has Our World Changed?

Read Together

Exploring the past will help us understand how our world has changed! We will learn about how people lived in the past and how life is different now.

HSS.K.6.3, HAS.CS.2, HAS.CS.3

(l)©Everett Historical/Shutterstock.com, (r)©Ariel Skelley/Blend Images/Corbis

How Do Things Change?

The way we do things has changed.

In the past, people listened to music on a large music player called a phonograph. Today, you can listen to music on a small music player!

past

present

Life Long Ago

(sung to the tune of "The Farmer in the Dell")

Before we were born,
Before we were here
Life was very different
In places far and near.

America was home
To native people, pioneers.
They lived long before us.
What did they do here?

Thinkstock Images/Stockbyte/Getty Images

They didn't ride in cars.

They didn't watch TV.

Life has really changed a lot.

It's plain for us to see.

So who lived right here?

And who traveled there?

Let's read and listen now.

There's such a lot to share!

Think About It

1. When was "long ago"? Who lived in America then?

2. How was life different long ago?

How Did People Live Long Ago?

Read Together

Homes Have Changed

Long ago life was different.

People made food over a fire.

Today we make food on a stove.

fireplace

stove

(l)Marzolino/Shutterstock.com; (r)elenaleonova/iStock/Getty Images

HSS.K.6.3, HAS.CS.2, HAS.CS.3, HAS.HR.1

candle

lamp

In the past, people used candles for light.

Today we use lamps.

✓ Stop and Check

COLLABORATE

Perspectives What do the pictures tell you about life in the past? How is life today different from life in the past?

How Has Clothing Changed?

Clothing has changed too!

Look at the picture.

How are the clothes like
yours? How are they different?

PRIMARY SOURCE

✓ Stop and Check

COLLABORATE

Make Connections How are clothes from the past like clothes you wear today? How are they different?

What Was Life Like When You Were a Child?

Sam asked his grandma to tell him about her life as a child.

"In the morning I walked to school.

We played hopscotch at recess.

After school I helped at home.

I washed the dishes.

I listened to the radio with my family."

✓ Stop and Check

COLLABORATE

Make Connections How is your life like the grandmother's life as a child? How is your life different?

What Do You Think?

What was life like long ago?

How Do Communities Change?

Read Together

How Have Schools Changed?

This is a school long ago.

It was made of wood.

PRIMARY SOURCE

a school long ago

Library of Congress Prints and Photographs Division, [LC-USZ62-59648]

HSS.K.1.2, HSS.K.4.5, HSS.K.6.2, HSS.K.6.3, HAS.CS.3, HAS.HR.1, HAS.HI.1, HAS.HI.2

The school had one classroom.

Children of all ages learned together.

The school had only one teacher.

How is it like your classroom?

PRIMARY SOURCE

a classroom long ago

This is a school today.

It is made of bricks.

Does this school look like yours?

© Steve Geer

This school has many classrooms.

Children learn with others who are the same age.

There are many teachers in the school.

✓ **Stop and Check** COLLABORATE

Talk How have schools changed? How have they stayed the same?

Who was Ruby Bridges?

Long ago, some communities did not allow white and black children to go to the same school.

Many people said this law needed to change.

Ruby Bridges and her family helped change this law.

In first grade, Ruby was chosen to be one of the first black children to attend an all-white school.

Some people did not want Ruby to go to this school.

Ruby was very brave.

She kept going to school.

Finally, Ruby and others went to schools with both white and black children.

Ruby Bridges
at school

✓ Stop and Check

COLLABORATE

Perspectives How did Ruby Bridges change school? Why do you think what Ruby did was important?

How Have Firefighters Changed?

Long ago horses pulled a fire engine with water in it.
Volunteers used buckets to put out fires.

a fire engine long ago

Today some communities still have volunteer firefighters.

They use trucks with hoses to put out fires.

Stockbyte/Getty Images

a fire engine today

☑ Stop and Check

Perspectives How do the changes help firefighters do their job better?

What Do You Think?

How have communities changed?

Read Together

Bicycles change!

Bicycles have been around for over 200 years.

Long ago, bikes looked very different.

Some had huge front wheels.
Some looked like a big tricycle.

Now they are made in all different sizes.

There are over a billion bicycles in the world!

Library of Congress Prints & Photographs Division (LC-USZ62-105442)

HSS.K.4.2, HSS.K.4.3, HSS.K.6.2, HSS.K.6.3, HAS.CS.1, HAS.CS.3, HAS.CS.4, HAS.HR.1, HAS.HR.2

✓ Stop and Check

COLLABORATE

Perspectives What do you think it would be like to travel long ago? How is **transportation** different now?

How Have Maps Changed?

This **map** is a drawing of a place.

This is a map of San Francisco from 1908.

Long ago maps were drawn on paper.

Today maps can be paper or digital.

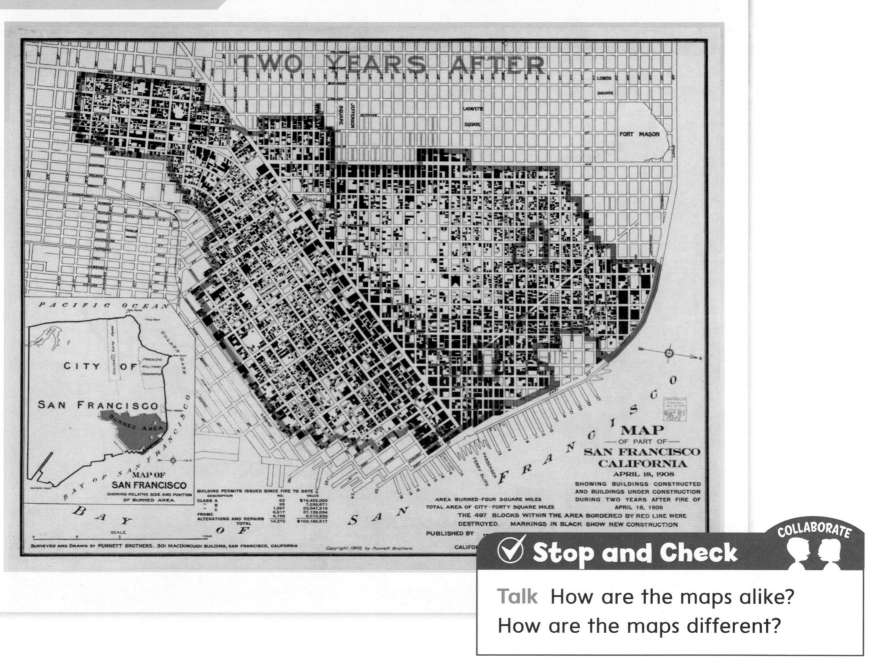

TWO YEARS AFTER

MAP
—OF PART OF—
SAN FRANCISCO
CALIFORNIA
APRIL 18, 1908

SHOWING BUILDINGS CONSTRUCTED
AND BUILDINGS UNDER CONSTRUCTION
DURING TWO YEARS AFTER FIRE OF
APRIL 18, 1906
THE 497 BLOCKS WITHIN THE AREA BORDERED BY RED LINE WERE
DESTROYED.   MARKINGS IN BLACK SHOW NEW CONSTRUCTION

Stop and Check

COLLABORATE

Talk How are the maps alike?
How are the maps different?

Who was Laura Ingalls Wilder?

Laura Ingalls Wilder was born on February 7, 1867.

She was born in Wisconsin.

Her family lived in several other states, too.

Laura's family traveled in a wagon.

The wagon carried all their things.

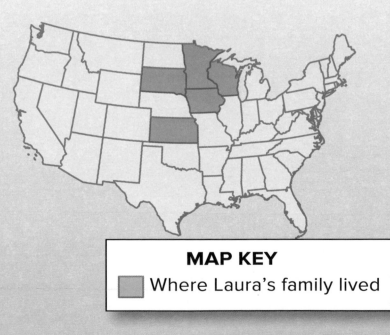

MAP KEY

⬛ Where Laura's family lived

Laura Ingalls Wilder

a covered wagon

✓ Stop and Check

COLLABORATE

Find Where did Laura live?

Talk How might Laura's family travel today?

What Do You Think?

How has travel changed?

How Has Our Nation Changed?

Read Together The First Americans

American Indians lived long, long ago right where you live now.

They were the first people to live in our country.

Later people started to explore the **world**.

People from Europe came to America.

Photos.com/Getty Images

Where in the World?

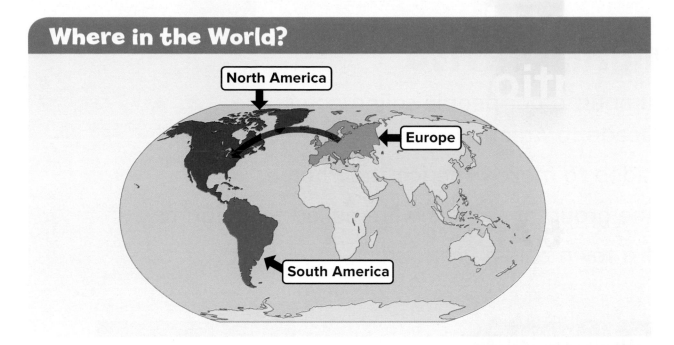

Christopher Columbus was one of the first people from Europe to come to America.

Many other people came after him.

Perspectives Why do you think people explored the world?

The Pilgrims Arrive

After Columbus, other people sailed across the Atlantic Ocean to America.

Many decided to make America their home.

In 1620, one group of settlers were called the Pilgrims.

They built a town called Plymouth.

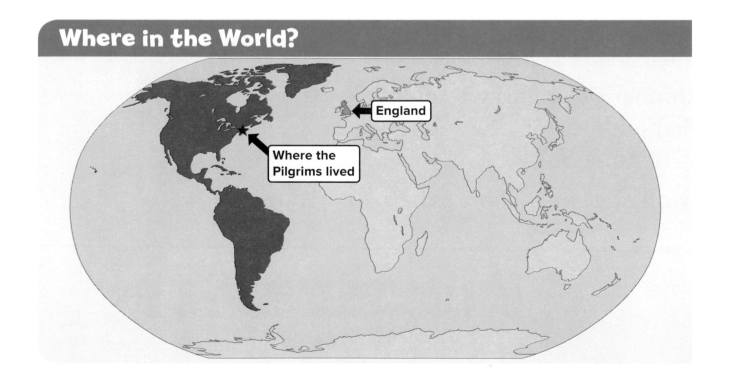

Where in the World?

England

Where the Pilgrims lived

Pilgrims in America

✓ **Stop and Check**

COLLABORATE

Perspectives Why are the Pilgrims important to America?

The First Thanksgiving

The Pilgrims first winter was cold.

They had little food.

The Pilgrims planted seeds. The seeds did not grow.

The American Indians helped. They showed the Pilgrims how to grow food.

the first Thanksgiving

Barney Burstein/Corbis Historical/Getty Images

Today Thanksgiving is a **holiday** that we celebrate in our country.

✓ Stop and Check

COLLABORATE

Talk How was the first Thanksgiving celebration like Thanksgiving celebrations today? How was it different?

What Do You Think?

How has our nation changed?

fstop123/Getty Images

What Can We Learn from the Past?

Why was Pocahontas Important?

Pocahontas lived in Virginia long ago.

She was the daughter of Chief Powhatan of the Pamunkey people.

She met English settlers who came to Jamestown in 1607.

Pocahontas carried messages between her people and the settlers.

PRIMARY SOURCE

Library of Congress Prints and Photographs Division (LC-D416-151)

HSS.K.1.2, HSS.K.4.2, HSS.K.6.2, HAS.CS.1, HAS.CS.2, HAS.CS.4, HAS.HR.1, HAS.HI.1, HAS.HI.3

Where in the World?

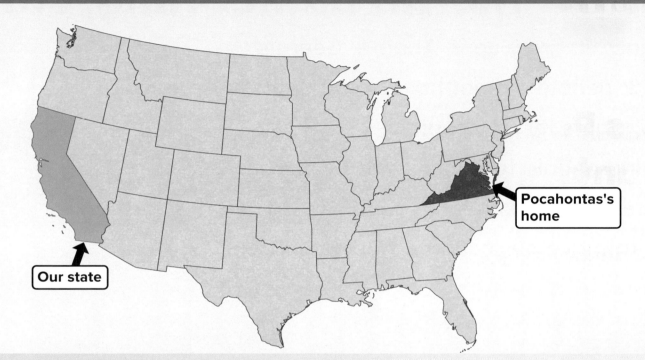

Pocahontas's home

Our state

Pocahontas helped them trade food.

She showed them how to cooperate.

In 1614, Pocahontas married an Englishman named John Rolfe.

✓ **Stop and Check** COLLABORATE

Find Where did Pocahontas live? Find where she lived on the map.

Perspectives What did Pocahontas teach people?

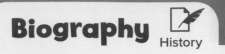
Who was Dr. Martin Luther King, Jr.?

Martin Luther King, Jr. grew up in Atlanta, Georgia.

He saw that black people did not have equal rights in America.

He wanted equal rights for all people.

He wanted to bring people together.

Dr. King had a dream that all people could live and work together.

He worked hard to make our country a better place.

Dr. King is a hero.

PRIMARY SOURCE

In Their Words... Martin Luther King, Jr.

"...time is always right to do right."

—Martin Luther King, Jr.

Reprinted by arrangement with The Heirs to the Estate of Martin Luther King Jr., c/o Writers House as agent for the proprietor New York, NY. Copyright 1965 Dr. Martin Luther King Jr; copyright renewed 1991 Coretta Scott King

PRIMARY SOURCE

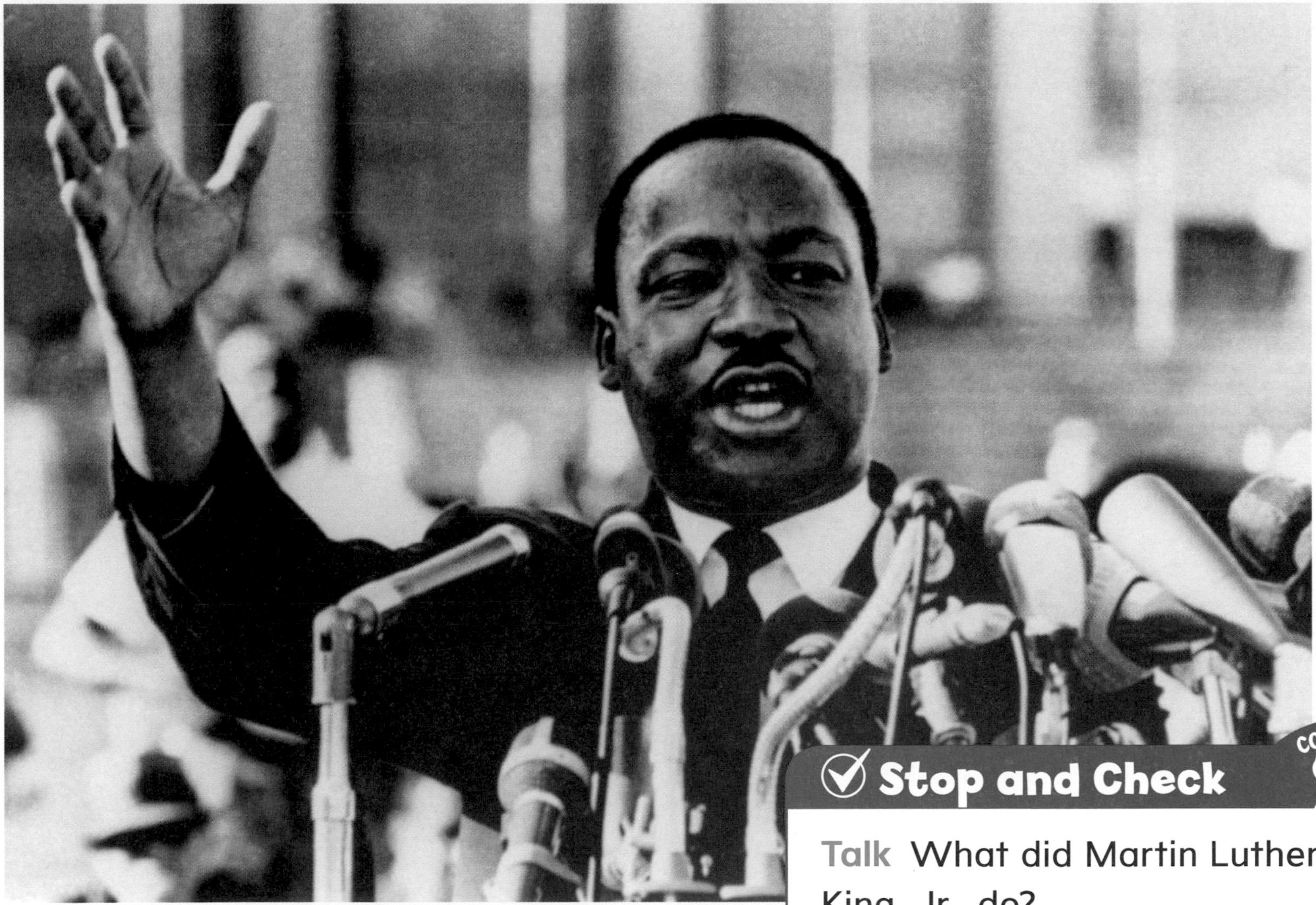

Glasshouse Images/Alamy

Stop and Check

COLLABORATE

Talk What did Martin Luther King, Jr., do?

Perspectives How can we learn from what King did?

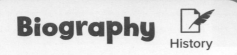
Fight for Freedom

Many years ago, there were unfair laws.

One law said that black people had to sit at the back of the bus.

Rosa Parks knew this was not fair.

She wanted to change that law.

PRIMARY SOURCE

Rosa Parks on a bus

Don Cravens/The LIFE Images Collection/Getty Images

In 1955 Rosa Parks would not give up her front seat to a white man. The police arrested her.

Dr. King and other people saw what Rosa did. They helped her fight for freedom.

Finally, the United States Supreme Court said the law was unfair.

People could sit anywhere they wanted on buses.

Rosa Parks

✓ Stop and Check COLLABORATE

Talk Why was Rosa Parks important?

Connect to Self How can you be more like Rosa Parks?

What Do You Think?

What can you learn from people in our country's **past**?

Connections in Action!
Back to the Essential Question

Think about the chapter question, **"How has our world changed?"**

Talk with a partner about life long ago and today. What did you learn about life in the past? How is life different now? Share your ideas with the class.

More to Explore

How Can You Make an IMPACT?

Who Am I?

You've learned about people from the past. Get together with a partner. Take turns pretending you are someone you learned about. You will give clues to help your partner guess who you are. You will guess who your partner is.

We Have a Past!

Think about things that happened in your own past. What did you like to do when you were little? What special memories do you have? Draw a picture of your past. Put your picture up in the classroom for everyone to see!

Draw the Word

Get together with a partner. Take turns naming a word you learned in this chapter. Your partner will draw to show the words you name. You will draw the words your partner names.

Why Do People Work?

Exploring jobs will help us learn more about people in our community. We will learn about work we do at school. We will also learn about how we can make good choices.

HSS.K.3, HAS.HI.2

elenaleonova/iStock/Getty Images

What Is My Job?

People have jobs to do!

I am a babysitter. I help take care of children.

I am a student. I learn about the world around me.

I am a baker. I make food for people to eat.

Busy City

by Rachel Young,
art by Claude Martinot

Ten speedy skaters rolling down the trails,
Nine wiggly puppies chasing balls and tails,
Eight tired travelers waiting for the bus,
Seven little babies about to make a fuss,
Six yellow taxicabs idling at the light,

3 HOT PRETZELS, PLEASE.

Five window washers who aren't afraid of heights,

Four blue balloons bouncing in the breeze,

Three best friends saying, "Three hot pretzels, please,"

Two gray pigeons sharing pretzel treats,

One dancing drummer banging out the beat,

To the buzzing, honking, humming of a busy city street.

Think About It

1. What can you see in the busy city?
2. What can you hear in the busy city?
3. Why do you think the title of this poem is "Busy City"?

People You Should Know

Pat Mora

Pat Mora is a writer. Her job is to write books for children and adults. Many of the characters in her books are Hispanic, just like her!

kittimages/iStockphoto/Getty Images

Yo-Yo Ma

Yo-Yo Ma is a musician. He plays
an instrument called the cello.
He plays music in front of big
groups of people!

How Do We Work at School?

Read Together

Jobs at School

All jobs are not the same.

You have a job at school.

Your job is to learn.

Your job is to cooperate with others.

It is important to do a good job, whatever you do.

FatCamera/E+/Getty Images

✓ **Stop and Check**

COLLABORATE

Make Connections What is your job at school?

What Do We Do at School?

first

later

next

last

then

✓ Stop and Check

COLLABORATE

Talk Retell the events on the timeline in order.

Make Connections How are the events the same as your school day? How are the events different?

How Can We Be Responsible?

Read about how these kindergarteners do their work at school.

We follow rules.

We are kind to each other.

We are responsible.

We do our work.

We clean up.

We work at school!

✓ Stop and Check

COLLABORATE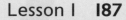

Make Connections What can you do to be responsible at school?

Volunteers

Some people work without making money.

They are called volunteers.

They like to help others.

Mrs. Vasques is a volunteer. She is an artist.

She volunteers at a school.

Poznyakov/Shutterstock.com

Some volunteers work to help children read and write.

✓ Stop and Check

Talk How do volunteers help others?

What Do You Think?

How do we work at school?

What Are Needs and Wants?

What Are Needs?

Needs are things we must have to live. We need food to eat, water to drink, and clothes to wear. People need a shelter too. A shelter is where someone lives.

HSS.K.1.2, HSS.K.1.3

What Are Wants?

Wants are things we do not need. We cannot have everything we want. We have to make choices.

✓ Stop and Check

COLLABORATE

Talk How are wants and needs different?

Money

People earn money for the work they do. People use money to buy things they need and want.

Money can be paper bills or coins.

©McGraw-Hill Education

Sometimes we want to buy something but we do not have enough money.

There is something we can do about it! We can save our money. To save means to put it away to use later.

Danny wants to buy new skates. He can save money in his bank. Soon he will have enough to buy new skates.

✓ **Stop and Check** COLLABORATE

Talk How do people earn money? How do people use money?

Making Choices

Lin has five dollars. She wants to buy a new toy.

A flow chart shows the order in which things happen.

This flow chart shows how Lin made her decision.

Lin wants to buy a toy.

Lin looks at her choices.

Lin made her choice and has a dollar to put in her bank.

✓ **Stop and Check** COLLABORATE

Perspectives Did Lin make a good choice? Why or why not?

The Ant and the Grasshopper

What Do You Think?

What are needs and wants?

What Jobs Are Part of a Community?

How Do Community Workers Help Us?

There are many workers in our community.
Community helpers make our world a better place.
A street cleaner helps keep our roads clean.

HSS.K.3

An ambulance driver helps people get to the hospital.

A sanitation worker takes away trash.

✓ **Stop and Check**

COLLABORATE

Perspectives Why are these jobs important?

Who Works in These Places?

Doctors and nurses work here.
They help people who are sick or hurt.

Librarians work here.
They help people find books.

hospital

library

Grocery clerks work here.

They keep the store filled with food.

Firefighters keep their trucks here.

They use the tools on their trucks to help put out fires.

grocery store

fire station

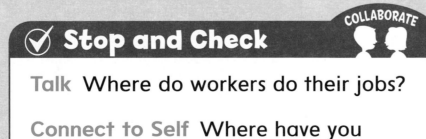

✓ Stop and Check   COLLABORATE

Talk Where do workers do their jobs?

Connect to Self Where have you seen workers in our community?

What Do You Think?

What jobs help our community?

The United States Post Office

The official United States Postal Service started on July 26, 1775. Benjamin Franklin was the first United States Postmaster.

In 1860, a new mail service started. It was called the Pony Express. It was a mail service between St. Joseph, Missouri, and Sacramento, California. That's 1900 miles!

1775

1860

(l)Courtesy National Gallery of Art, Washington; (r)Library of Congress Prints and Photographs Division (LC-USZC4-2458)

There are 40,000 post offices in our country. Mail carriers are important community helpers!

Today

BassittART/E+/Getty Images

What Do You Think?
What jobs help our community?

How Have Jobs Changed Over Time?

Farming Changes Too!

Long ago people had to work very hard to grow food.

They dug up the ground with shovels.

They planted seeds with their hands.

This took a long time!

Many farmers used a horse and plow.

The horse pulled the plow to break up the dirt.

This was a little bit faster!

Photo by B.C. McLean, USDA Natural Resources Conservation Service

HSS.K.3, HSS.K.6.3, HAS.CS.3, HAS.HR.1

Today, farmers use tractors to dig the ground.
They use machines to plant the seeds.
Machines make our work better and
much faster.

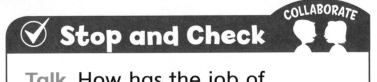

✓ **Stop and Check** COLLABORATE

Talk How has the job of
farming changed?

People With Great Ideas

In 1876, Alexander Graham Bell had a great idea!

He made the very first telephone.

Many years ago, telephones were big and heavy.

A cord connected the handset to the base of the phone.

People could not take their phone out of their home.

(l)Photos.com/Getty Images; (r)Ingram Publishing/SuperStock

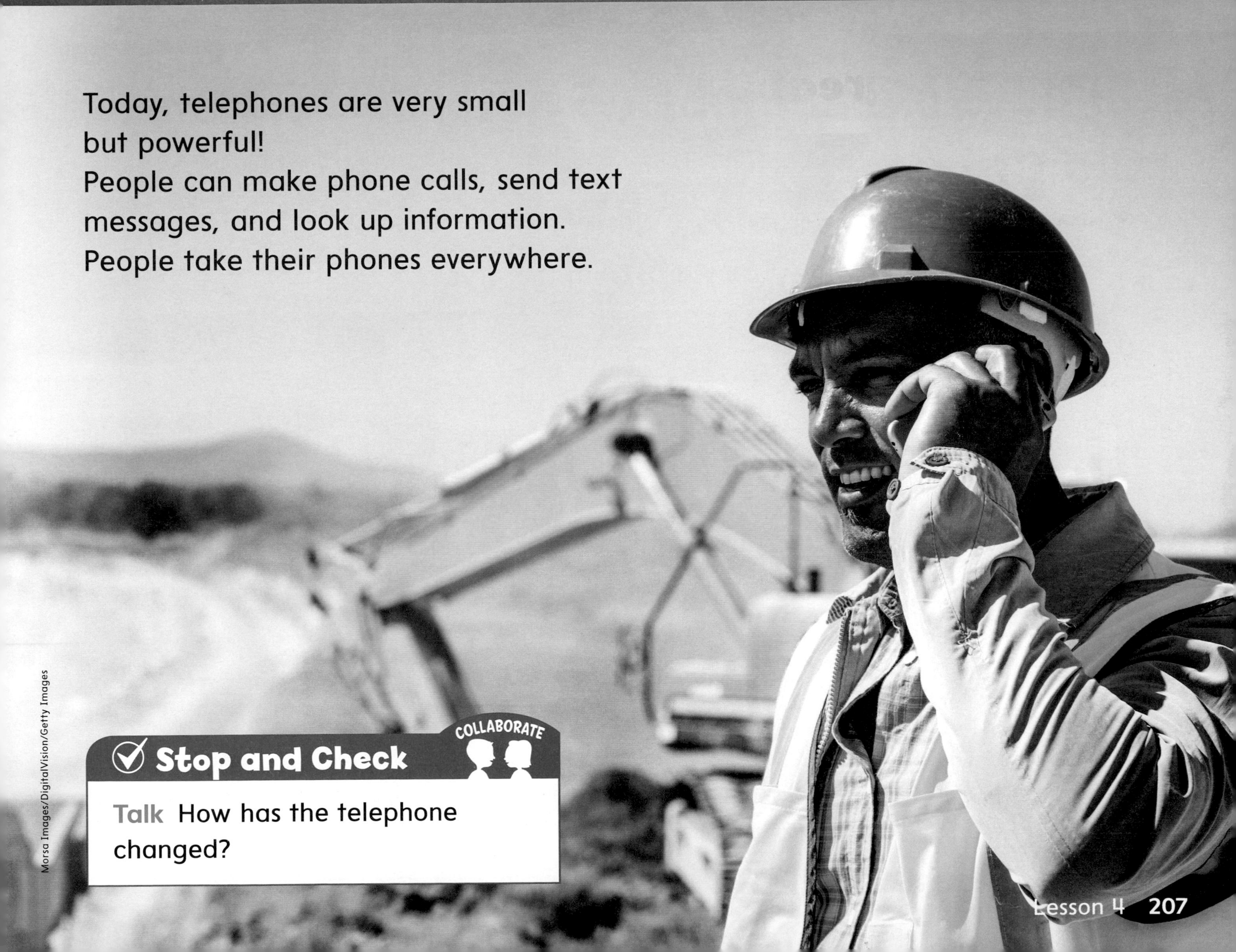

Today, telephones are very small but powerful!
People can make phone calls, send text messages, and look up information.
People take their phones everywhere.

✓ **Stop and Check**

COLLABORATE

Talk How has the telephone changed?

What kinds of jobs do you do at home?

I help my father fold our laundry!

I love it when the clothes are warm from the dryer.

I help my mom with making dinner.

✓ **Stop and Check** COLLABORATE

Make Connections

What job do you do at home?

What Do You Think?

How have jobs changed?

What Kinds of Jobs Do People Have?

Read Together

Making Goods

Goods are things that people grow or make to sell. Farmers grow good like flowers, beans, corn, and strawberries to sell.

ricardoazoury/Vetta/Getty Images

Some goods are made in a building called a factory. Factory workers run machines to make the goods.

☑ **Stop and Check** COLLABORATE

Talk What are goods?

People with Great Ideas!

People with great ideas help make our work and lives better.

George Washington Carver grew up on a farm in Diamond Grove, Missouri. He discovered over 100 ways to use peanuts!

Where in the World?

Missouri

Did You Know?

It takes over 500 peanuts to make one jar of peanut butter!

PRIMARY SOURCE

In Their Words... Ellen Ochoa

"Working so closely with a team to accomplish a challenging, meaningful task is the greatest reward of being an astronaut."

—Ellen Ochoa

Ellen Ochoa made a tool that helps robot arms move in space. She later became on astronaut. She worked hard in school.

✓ Stop and Check   COLLABORATE

Talk Talk How did Ellen Ochoa's invention make work easier?

Jobs Around the World

These artists are in South Africa.

They make pots and other things out of clay.

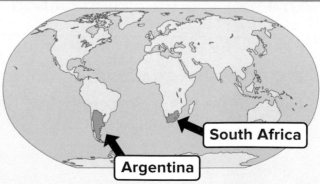

Where in the World?

South Africa

Argentina

(bkgd)Greatstock/Alamy, (inset)D Guest Smith/Alamy

Architects draw the plans for buildings.

There are architects all over the world.

These architects are in Argentina.

They working with the construction workers to build a new building.

✓ Stop and Check

Talk How are workers around the world alike?

Kids at Work!

What are some jobs that children can do?

(l)JACKY YEUNG/iStock/Getty images; (c)Don Hammond/Design Pics; (r)Caia Image/Glow Images

What Do You Think?

What kinds of jobs do people have?

Connections in Action!

Back to the Essential Question

Think about the chapter question, **"Why do people work?"**

Talk with a small group about the kinds of work you read about in this chapter. What workers have you seen in our community? What do the workers do? Draw a list of the workers. Share your list with the class.

SelectStock/Vetta/Getty Images

More to Explore

How Can You Make an IMPACT?

Words for Workers

Get together with a partner. Take turns naming a worker you have learned about. Say words that remind you of the worker, such as *carrot* or *cow* for a farmer.

My Needs and Wants

Think about things you need and want. Draw pictures of three things you need. Draw pictures of three things you want. Label your pictures. Then put the pages together to make a book of your needs and wants!

Where Do They Work?

Get together with a small group. Talk about the places where workers do their jobs. Build a model of a community with the places you talked about. Then share your model with the class. Tell who works in each place.

Reference Sources

The Reference Sources has many parts, each with a different type of information. Use this section to explore people, places, and events as you investigate and take action.

Holidays

We celebrate many holidays. Holidays are days when we celebrate special people and events. They are times to celebrate our families and communities. Celebrating holidays reminds us how to be good citizens.

Martin Luther King, Jr., Day

We celebrate Martin Luther King, Jr., Day in January. Martin Luther King, Jr., worked hard to make our laws fair. On this day, we remember how Martin Luther King Jr., made America a better place.

Presidents' Day

In February, we celebrate Presidents' Day. This special day helps us remember the people who were Presidents of the United States.

Flag Day

We celebrate Flag Day on June 14. On that day long ago, our country chose its first flag. Today, our flag has fifty stars that stand for the fifty states in our country. To celebrate Flag Day, we fly the American flag.

Independence Day

Independence Day is on July 4. It celebrates the birthday of the United States of America. We celebrate with parades. We also watch fireworks.

Veterans Day

On November 11, we celebrate Veterans Day.
A veteran is a person who has protected our
country. A veteran is a hero.

Thanksgiving

Thanksgiving is celebrated in November. On this day we remember the feast shared by the Pilgrims and the American Indians. We celebrate by sharing a special meal with family and friends. We give thanks for what we have.

The Themes of Geography

You can think of geography in five parts. Each part is a theme. These themes help us learn about geography.

Location

A location tells where a place is on Earth. Your home address is a location.

Place

There are many kinds of places on Earth. Roads, cities, and mountains are all places.

Region

A region is a bigger area than a place. A region shares the same weather and landforms.

Movement

There is movement when people go from place to place. The ways that people move can change the land and air.

People Change the Land

People build roads, houses, and parks. The things people build change the land.

Dictionary of Geographic Words

Desert Hot, dry area that has few plants

Hill Land that is higher than the land around it, but not as high as a mountain

Lake Body of water with land all around it

Peninsula Land that has water on all sides but one

Island Land that has water all around it

Ocean Largest body of water

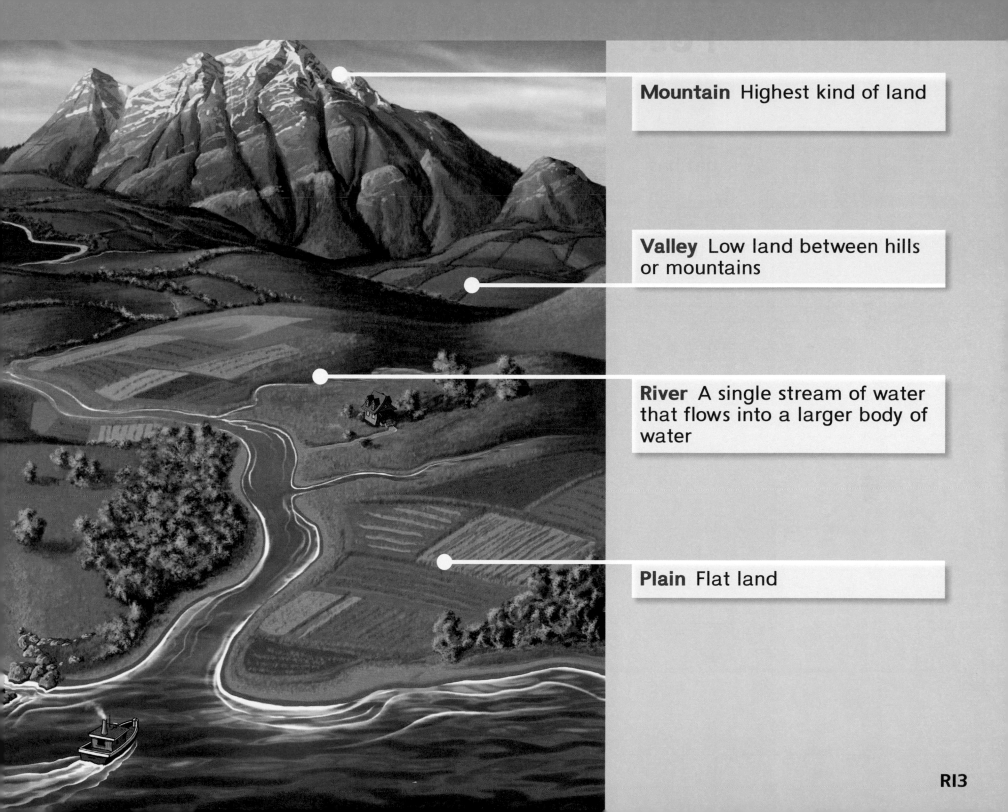

Mountain Highest kind of land

Valley Low land between hills or mountains

River A single stream of water that flows into a larger body of water

Plain Flat land

The United States

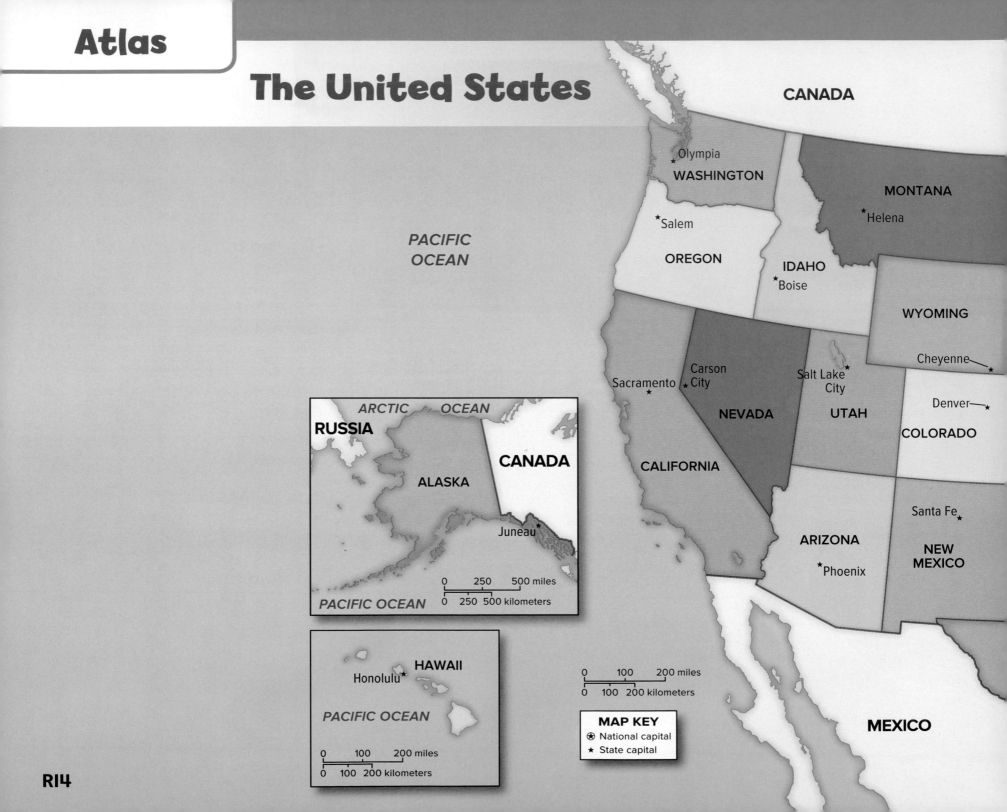

CANADA

★ Olympia
WASHINGTON

★ Salem

PACIFIC OCEAN

OREGON

MONTANA
★ Helena

IDAHO
★ Boise

WYOMING

Cheyenne ★

★ Sacramento

Carson
★ City

Salt Lake ★
City

Denver ★

NEVADA

UTAH

COLORADO

CALIFORNIA

Santa Fe ★

ARIZONA

NEW MEXICO

★ Phoenix

ARCTIC OCEAN

RUSSIA

CANADA

ALASKA

Juneau ★

| 0 | 250 | 500 miles |
| 0 | 250 | 500 kilometers |

PACIFIC OCEAN

HAWAII

Honolulu ★

PACIFIC OCEAN

| 0 | 100 | 200 miles |
| 0 | 100 | 200 kilometers |

| 0 | 100 | 200 miles |
| 0 | 100 | 200 kilometers |

MEXICO

MAP KEY
⊛ National capital
★ State capital

CANADA

Lake
Superior

MINNESOTA

NORTH
DAKOTA
Bismarck

SOUTH
DAKOTA
Pierre

St. Paul

WISCONSIN
Madison

MICHIGAN
Lake
Huron

Lansing

Lake
Michigan

Lake
Ontario

Lake
Erie

NEW
HAMPSHIRE
VERMONT
Montpelier

MAINE
Augusta

Concord
Boston
MASSACHUSETTS
Providence
RHODE ISLAND
CONNECTICUT

Albany

NEW YORK

Hartford

NEBRASKA
Lincoln

IOWA
Des
Moines

ILLINOIS
Springfield

INDIANA

Indianapolis

OHIO
Columbus

PENNSYLVANIA

Harrisburg

Trenton
NEW JERSEY

Washington, D.C.

Dover
DELAWARE
Annapolis
MARYLAND

WEST
VIRGINIA
Charleston

Richmond

KANSAS
Topeka

Jefferson
City

MISSOURI

KENTUCKY
Frankfort

VIRGINIA

OKLAHOMA
Oklahoma
City

ARKANSAS
Little
Rock

TENNESSEE
Nashville

NORTH
CAROLINA
Raleigh

Columbia
SOUTH
CAROLINA

TEXAS

Austin

LOUISIANA

Baton Rouge

MISSISSIPPI
Jackson

ALABAMA

Montgomery

GEORGIA

Atlanta

ATLANTIC
OCEAN

Tallahassee

FLORIDA

THE
BAHAMAS

Gulf of Mexico

N
W   E
S

The World

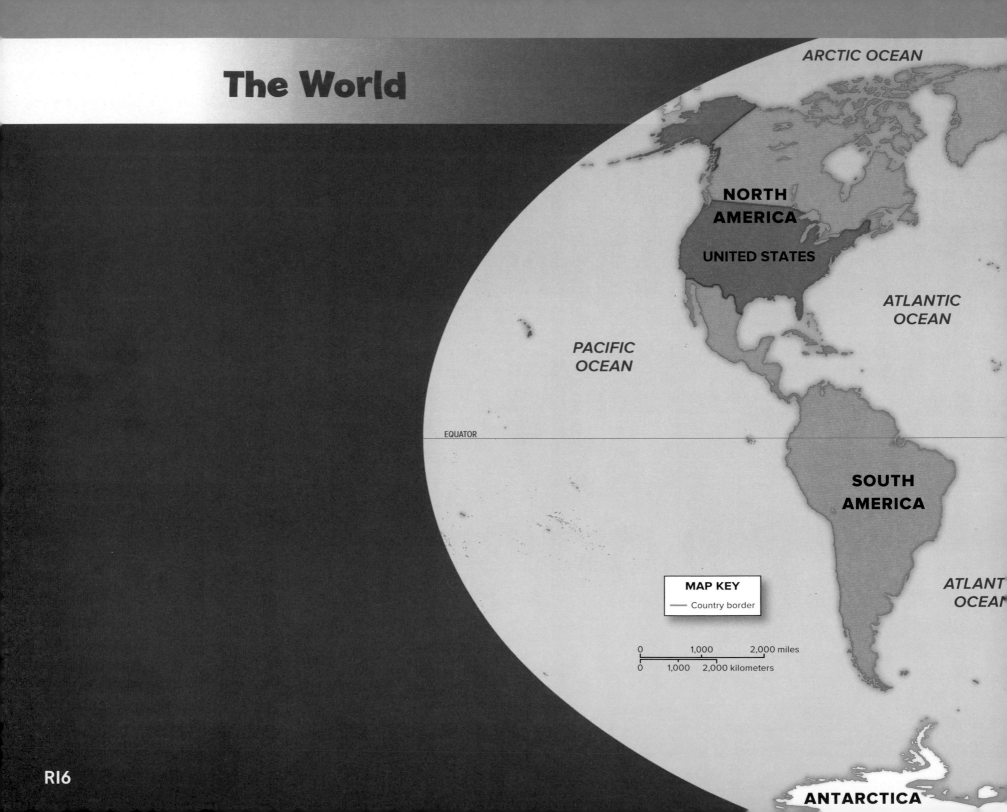

ARCTIC OCEAN

NORTH
AMERICA

UNITED STATES

PACIFIC
OCEAN

ATLANTIC
OCEAN

EQUATOR

SOUTH
AMERICA

MAP KEY
—— Country border

ATLANT
OCEAN

0   1,000   2,000 miles

0   1,000   2,000 kilometers

ANTARCTICA

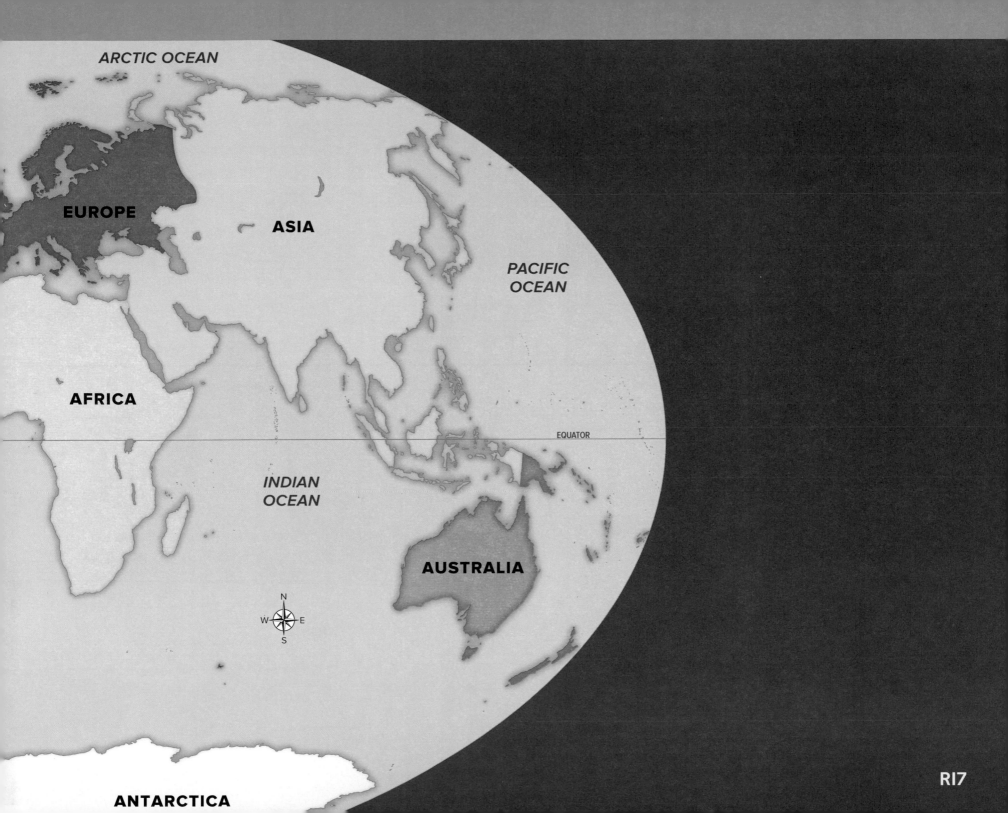

ARCTIC OCEAN

EUROPE

ASIA

PACIFIC
OCEAN

AFRICA

INDIAN
OCEAN

EQUATOR

AUSTRALIA

N
W   E
S

ANTARCTICA

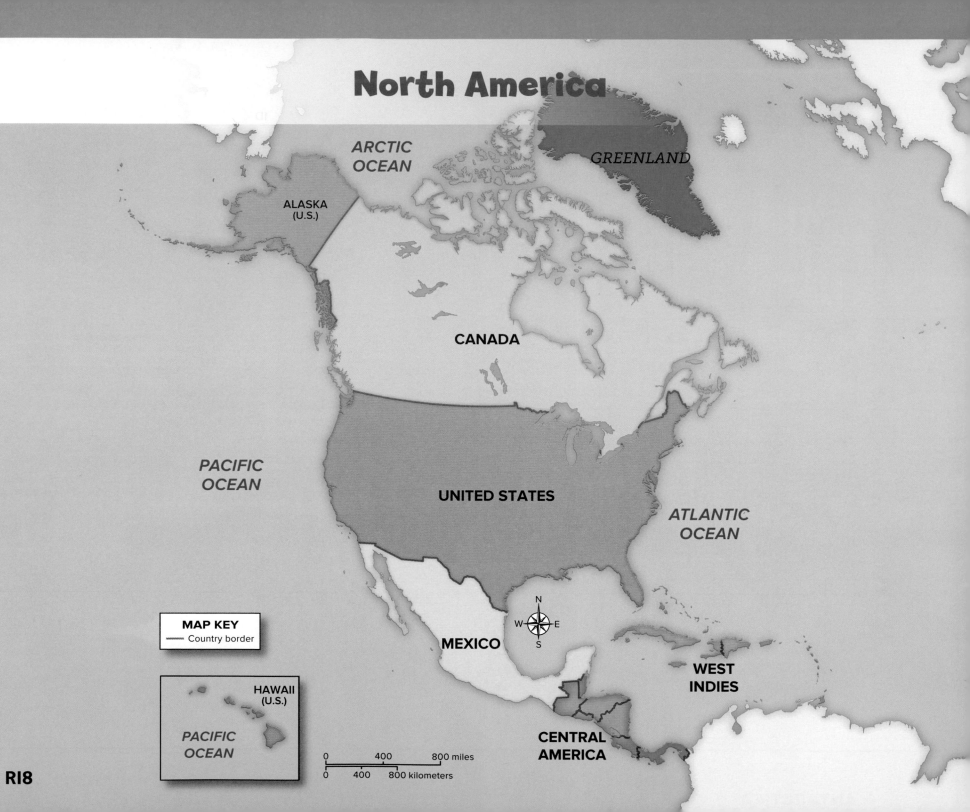

North America

ARCTIC OCEAN

GREENLAND

ALASKA (U.S.)

CANADA

PACIFIC OCEAN

UNITED STATES

ATLANTIC OCEAN

MAP KEY
Country border

MEXICO

N
W E
S

WEST INDIES

HAWAII (U.S.)

PACIFIC OCEAN

CENTRAL AMERICA

0   400   800 miles
0   400   800 kilometers

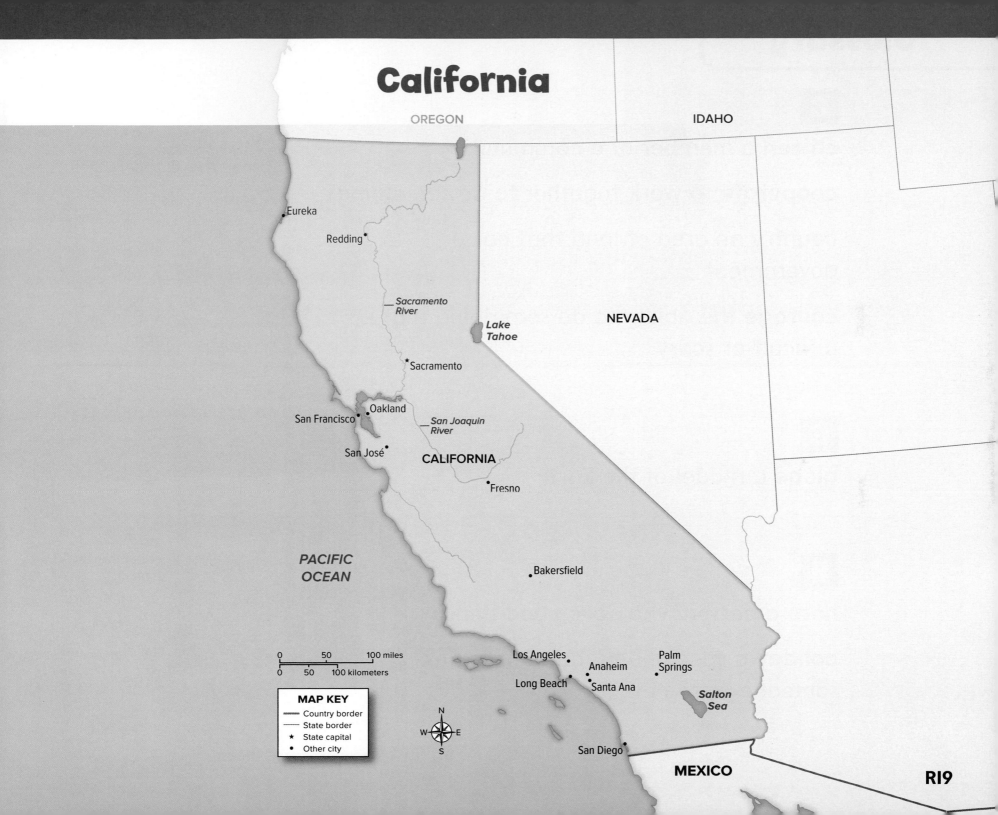

California

OREGON

IDAHO

NEVADA

Eureka

Redding

Sacramento River

Lake Tahoe

★ Sacramento

Oakland

San Francisco

San Joaquin River

San José

CALIFORNIA

Fresno

PACIFIC OCEAN

Bakersfield

Los Angeles

Anaheim

Palm Springs

Long Beach

Santa Ana

Salton Sea

San Diego

MEXICO

R19

MAP KEY	
〰〰	Country border
——	State border
★	State capital
●	Other city

0 50 100 miles

0 50 100 kilometers

N W E S

Glossary

C

citizen a member of a community

cooperate to work together to do something

country an area of land that has a government

courage the ability to do something that is difficult or scary

G

globe a model of the Earth

H

hero a person who does good things

holiday a special day that celebrates someone or something

L

law a rule made by the government

M

map a picture that shows what is in an area

N

nation an area of land that has a government

need something a person must have

neighborhood a part of a town or city

P

past time long ago

present time now

R

responsibility something a person should do

right something a person gets

rule a statement that tells people how to act

S

state an area of a country

symbol something that stands for an idea

T

technology machines made with science

transportation a way of traveling from one place to another

V

volunteer a person who chooses to help

W

want something a person wishes to have

work the jobs that people do

world the Earth and all the people in it

Kindergarten
Historical and Social Sciences Content Standards and Analysis Skills

History-Social Science Content Standards.

Learning and Working Now and Long Ago

Students in kindergarten are introduced to basic spatial, temporal, and causal relationships, emphasizing the geographic and historical connections between the world today and the world long ago. The stories of ordinary and extraordinary people help describe the range and continuity of human experience and introduce the concepts of courage, self-control, justice, heroism, leadership, deliberation, and individual responsibility. Historical empathy for how people lived and worked long ago reinforces the concept of civic behavior: how we interact respectfully with each other, following rules, and respecting the rights of others.

K.I Students understand that being a good citizen involves acting in certain ways.

1. Follow rules, such as sharing and taking turns, and know the consequences of breaking them.
2. Learn examples of honesty, courage, determination, individual responsibility, and patriotism in American and world history from stories and folklore.
3. Know beliefs and related behaviors of characters in stories from times past and understand the consequences of the characters' actions.

K.2 Students recognize national and state symbols and icons such as the national and state flags, the bald eagle, and the Statue of Liberty.

K.3 Students match simple descriptions of work that people do and the names of related jobs at the school, in the local community, and from historical accounts.

K.4 Students compare and contrast the locations of people, places, and environments and describe their characteristics.

1. Determine the relative locations of objects using the terms near/far, left/right, and behind/in front.
2. Distinguish between land and water on maps and globes and locate general areas referenced in historical legends and stories.
3. Identify traffic symbols and map symbols (e.g., those for land, water, roads, cities).
4. Construct maps and models of neighborhoods, incorporating such structures as police and fire stations, airports, banks, hospitals, supermarkets, harbors, schools, homes, places of worship, and transportation lines.
5. Demonstrate familiarity with the school's layout, environs, and the jobs people do there.

K.5 Students put events in temporal order using a calendar, placing days, weeks, and months in proper order.

K.6 Students understand that history relates to events, people, and places of other times.

1. Identify the purposes of, and the people and events honored in, commemorative holidays, including the human struggles that were the basis for the events (e.g., Thanksgiving, Independence Day, Washington's and Lincoln's Birthdays, Martin Luther King Jr. Day, Memorial Day, Labor Day, Columbus Day, Veterans Day).
2. Know the triumphs in American legends and historical accounts through the stories of such people as Pocahontas, George Washington, Booker T. Washington, Daniel Boone, and Benjamin Franklin.
3. Understand how people lived in earlier times and how their lives would be different today (e.g., getting water from a well, growing food, making clothing, having fun, forming organizations, living by rules and laws).

Historical and Social Sciences Analysis Skills

In addition to the standards, students demonstrate the following intellectual, reasoning, reflection, and research skills:

Chronological and Spatial Thinking

1. Students place key events and people of the historical era they are studying in a chronological sequence and within a spatial context; they interpret time lines.
2. Students correctly apply terms related to time, including past, present, future, decade, century, and generation.
3. Students explain how the present is connected to the past, identifying both similarities and differences between the two, and how some things change over time and some things stay the same.
4. Students use map and globe skills to determine the absolute locations of places and interpret information available through a map's or globe's legend, scale, and symbolic representations.
5. Students judge the significance of the relative location of a place (e.g., proximity to a harbor, on trade routes) and analyze how relative advantages or disadvantages can change over time.

Research, Evidence, and Point of View

1. Students differentiate between primary and secondary sources.
2. Students pose relevant questions about events they encounter in historical documents, eyewitness accounts, oral histories, letters, diaries, artifacts, photographs, maps, artworks, and architecture.
3. Students distinguish fact from fiction by comparing documentary sources on historical figures and events with fictionalized characters and events.

Historical Interpretation

1. Students summarize the key events of the era they are studying and explain the historical contexts of those events.
2. Students identify the human and physical characteristics of the places they are studying and explain how those features form the unique character of those places.
3. Students identify and interpret the multiple causes and effects of historical events.
4. Students conduct cost-benefit analyses of historical and current events.